THE PACIFICUS-HELVIDIUS DEBATES OF 1793–1794

James Madison

Alexander Hamilton

The
Pacificus-Helvidius
Debates of
1793–1794

Toward the Completion of the American Founding

Alexander Hamilton
AND James Madison

Edited and with an
Introduction by Morton J. Frisch

LIBERTY FUND
Indianapolis

This book is published by Liberty Fund, Inc., a foundation established to encourage study of the ideal of a society of free and responsible individuals.

𒂷𒄑 𒉽𒌍

The cuneiform inscription that serves as our logo and as the design motif for our endpapers is the earliest-known written appearance of the word "freedom" (*amagi*), or "liberty." It is taken from a clay document written about 2300 B.C. in the Sumerian city-state of Lagash.

11 10 09 08 07 C 5 4 3 2 1
11 10 09 08 07 P 5 4 3 2 1

Library of Congress Cataloging-in-Publication Data

Hamilton, Alexander, 1757–1804.
   The Pacificus-Helvidius debates of 1793–1794: toward the completion of the American founding/Alexander Hamilton and James Madison; edited and with an introduction by Morton J. Frisch.
       p.   cm.
   Includes bibliographical references and index.
   ISBN-13: 978-0-86597-688-7 (hardcover: alk. paper)
   ISBN-10: 0-86597-688-0 (hardcover: alk. paper)
   ISBN-13: 978-0-86597-689-4 (pbk.: alk. paper)
   ISBN-10: 0-86597-689-9 (pbk.: alk. paper)
       1. United States—Foreign relations—1789–1797.   2. United States—Politics and government—1789–1797.   3. Constitutional history—United States.   I. Madison, James, 1751–1836.   II. Frisch, Morton J.   III. Title.
   E313.H23   2007
   973.4—dc22   2006028280

Liberty Fund, Inc.
8335 Allison Pointe Trail, Suite 300
Indianapolis, Indiana 46250-1684

Contents

The Significance of the Pacificus–Helvidius Debates: Toward the Completion of the American Founding BY MORTON J. FRISCH   vii

Washington's Neutrality Proclamation, *April 22, 1793*   1

Defense of the President's Neutrality Proclamation
(Alexander Hamilton), *May 1793*   2

Pacificus Number I (Alexander Hamilton), *June 29, 1793*   8

Pacificus Number II (Alexander Hamilton), *July 3, 1793*   18

Pacificus Number III (Alexander Hamilton), *July 6, 1793*   26

Pacificus Number IV (Alexander Hamilton), *July 10, 1793*   30

Pacificus Number V (Alexander Hamilton), *July 13–17, 1793*   35

Pacificus Number VI (Alexander Hamilton), *July 17, 1793*   41

Pacificus Number VII (Alexander Hamilton), *July 27, 1793*   48

Thomas Jefferson to James Madison, *July 7, 1793*   54

Helvidius Number I (James Madison), *August 24, 1793*   55

Helvidius Number II (James Madison), *August 31, 1793*   65

Helvidius Number III (James Madison), *September 7, 1793*   74

Helvidius Number IV (James Madison), *September 14, 1793*   84

Helvidius Number V (James Madison), *September 18, 1793*   90

Americanus Number I (Alexander Hamilton), *January 31, 1794*   99

Americanus Number II (Alexander Hamilton), *February 7, 1794*   108

Index   117

The Significance of the Pacificus-Helvidius Debates: Toward the Completion of the American Founding

WASHINGTON's Neutrality Proclamation of 1793 had the effect of annulling the eleventh article of America's Treaty of Alliance with France of 1778. It involved a repudiation of obligations assumed by that treaty in response to France's declaration of war on Great Britain and Holland. That proclamation was criticized by the Jeffersonian faction in Congress as an encroachment on the powers of the Senate because the Senate has a right to be consulted in matters of foreign policy, and as an encroachment on the powers of Congress because it could, in effect, commit the nation to war without the consent of Congress. The Constitutional Convention had left largely undefined the precise manner in which legislative and executive authorities would share their divided responsibilities in the conduct of foreign relations; furthermore, the relation between executive power and republican government was not fully thought through and hence not completely worked out at that time.

The American Constitution was left uncompleted in 1789, for it needed additional making or doing. The most remarkable and perhaps least remarked-upon fact about that constitution at the time of its ratification was its unfinished character. In that uncertain founding, there was considerable debate about the limits of a limited constitution. It is in relation to the imbalances of the unfinished constitution (an unfinished constitution is neither an endlessly flexible constitution nor a constitution devoid of essential meaning) that Alexander Hamilton, James Madison, and Thomas

Jefferson set their courses to remodel the institutions of government in order to better secure the equilibrium which, in their view, that constitution intended. The controversies of the first Washington administration, which focused on the kinds of power that had been exercised (legislative and executive) and the degree to which power could be legitimately exercised, took the form of disputes over the way the Constitution should be construed.

When Jefferson read Hamilton's defense of Washington's Neutrality Proclamation in the newspapers, he virtually implored Madison to attack it. Although he had previously acquiesced in its issuance, it now became clear to him that Hamilton was using the neutrality issue to extend the area of executive control over foreign affairs. He wrote to Madison: "Nobody answers him, & his doctrine will therefore be taken for confessed. For God's sake, my dear Sir, take up your pen, select the most striking heresies, and cut him to pieces in the face of the public. There is nobody else who can & will enter the lists with him."[1] Madison, acting as Jefferson's surrogate, was in constant correspondence with him while composing his attack on Hamilton. We can therefore assume that Jefferson was in substantial agreement with the Madisonian arguments, arguments which were directed almost solely against the broad reach of executive power in foreign affairs. It was not the Neutrality Proclamation itself so much as the constitutional interpretation Hamilton advanced in its defense that was the object of their very great concern. Jefferson regarded it as particularly unfortunate that the Constitution left unresolved questions concerning the extent of executive power, especially in foreign affairs, and hence we can better understand why he reacted so strongly against Hamilton's broad construction of executive power. Madison, like Jefferson, favored the creation of an executive with vigorously limited powers, emphasizing that the president had not been given any specific power to declare neutrality as a policy. His alliance with Jefferson was formed, at least in part, to put an end to what was perceived as the monarchizing tendencies in the Hamiltonian programs and

1. Jefferson to Madison, July 7, 1793, *The Papers of James Madison*, ed. Thomas A. Mason, Robert A. Rutland, and Jeanne K. Sisson, vol. 15 (Charlottesville: University Press of Virginia, 1985), 43; and below, p. 54.

policies. They were convinced that it was his intention to create a virtually unlimited executive.

In the Pacificus letters Hamilton argued in support of Washington's proclamation that the president's power to make such a proclamation issues from the general grant of executive power in Article II of the Constitution, which (as he outlined it) includes conducting foreign relations; from the president's primary responsibility in the formation of treaties; and from the power of the execution of the laws, of which treaties form a part. He pointed out in Pacificus I that the first sentence of Article II of the Constitution, which declares that, "the executive power shall be vested in a President," was meant as a general grant of power, not merely a designation of office, despite the enumeration of executive powers in other sections of Article II, and that moreover this general grant leaves the full range of executive powers to be discovered by interpreting it "in conformity to other parts ⟨of⟩ the constitution and to the principles of free government."[2]

It would have been difficult for the Constitution to have contained "a complete and perfect specification of all the cases of Executive authority," Hamilton reasoned, and therefore it left a set of unspecified executive powers that must be determined by inference from the more comprehensive grant (Pacificus no. I, June 29, 1793, *Hamilton Papers*, 15:39; and below, p. 12). He maintained that the control over foreign affairs is, in its nature, an executive function and one which therefore belongs exclusively to the president in the absence of specific provisions to the contrary. He further argued that the power to declare war which the Constitution grants to Congress is an exception from the general grant of executive power, and as an exception, cannot diminish the president's authority in the exercise of those powers constitutionally granted to him.

Madison, the leader of the Jeffersonian faction in the Congress, objected that Hamilton's construction of Washington's proclamation as a neutrality proclamation constituted an infringement of the legislative power

---

2. Pacificus no. I, June 29, 1793, *The Papers of Alexander Hamilton*, ed. Harold Syrett et al., vol. 15 (New York: Columbia University Press, 1969), 38–39; and below, pp. 12–13.

since a proclamation of neutrality might practically foreclose Congress's option to wage war or not. Although Congress has the right to declare war, he argued that the president's claim of the right to judge national obligations under treaties could put Congress in a position in which it would find it difficult to exercise that right. Hamilton's answer was that the truth of this inference does not exclude the executive from a right of judgment in the execution of his own constitutional functions (Pacificus no. I, June 29, 1793, *Hamilton Papers*, 15:40; and below, p. 13). He admitted that the right of the executive, in certain cases, to determine the condition of the nation, by issuing a proclamation of neutrality, may affect the power of the legislature to declare war, but he saw that as no argument for constraining the executive in the carrying out of its functions (Pacificus no. I, June 29, 1793, *Hamilton Papers*, 15:42; and below, pp. 15–16). His argument was that the executive has broad authority in conducting foreign affairs, including the right to interpret treaties, declare peace or neutrality, and take actions that might later limit congressional options in declaring war.

But what about the Senate's involvement in treaties? This provision would seem to indicate that, at least with respect to one of the government's most important powers, the Constitution does not establish a government of simply separated powers, but a separation consistent with some mixture of legislating, executing, and judging—not too great a mixture, and only to prevent the abuses of power. The Constitution surely qualifies the separation of powers principle, for example, by qualifiedly granting the treaty-making power to the president. A qualified power is a power possessed by one official or one body which may be checked by another. But this does not suggest a constitutional intention of equal sharing; rather, it suggests the intention of qualifying the treaty-making power. In a very real sense, this power is not equally shared by the president and Senate, since the president is given the power of making treaties, whereas the Senate merely serves as check on the presidential power by virtue of the "advice and consent" provision. As a matter of fact, the treaty-making power is mentioned only in Article II; thus it is clearly executive despite the Senate's power to ratify treaties. Though the Senate is authorized to check the exercise of that power, the president remains responsible for its proper exercise.

In his Helvidius response, Madison referred to Hamilton's alleged admission in *Federalist* 75 that the treaty-making power was not essentially an executive power (Helvidius no. I, August 24, 1793, *Madison Papers*, 15:72–73; and below, pp. 63–64). Hamilton actually said that the treaty-making power is neither executive nor legislative in character, but seems to form a distinct department, what John Locke called the "federative power." But more important, Hamilton indicated that the executive is "the most fit agent" in "the management of foreign negotiations." He made it perfectly clear that the only reason for the Senate's participation in treaty making is that as the least numerous part of the legislative body, it provides a greater prospect for security; however, it has nothing to do with the actual exercise of negotiations. The Senate is given a very limited role in the formation of treaties—advice and consent—but not their negotiation, with the executive being in a position to determine the type and amount of advice it wishes to accept. In *Federalist* 75 Hamilton revealed the difficulty of classifying the treaty-making power as either an executive or legislative power. He suggested that the treaty-making power is federative, and that that, moreover, does not preclude the primacy of executive responsibility in exercising that function. Although that power is not primarily an executive function, the Constitution wisely places it in the class of executive authorities. Surely executive energy would not be impaired by legislative participation in the power of making treaties, since the Senate restrains only by virtue of concurring or not concurring with the executive's action.

Hamilton appeared to be much more a spokesman of limited government in *Federalist* 75, where he was discussing the participation of the Senate in treaty making, than in Pacificus I, where he was defending the president's exclusive authority to issue a neutrality proclamation. But the defense of the issuance of that proclamation, as previously indicated, is that the Senate's participation in treaty making is simply a qualification of the general grant of executive power to the president, that the Senate cannot claim an equal share in the exercise of that power, and that therefore the president has the exclusive right to determine the nature of the obligations which treaties impose upon the government, the Senate's power of advice and consent to the contrary notwithstanding. The president exercises the treaty-making power even though the Senate is provided with some check on that power.

Madison stressed the inconveniences and confusion likely to result from Hamilton's view of concurrent powers in the hands of different departments. He argued that "a concurrent authority in two independent departments to perform the same function with respect to the same thing, would be as awkward in practice, as it is unnatural in theory. If the legislature and executive have both a right to judge of the obligations to make war or not, it must sometimes happen, though not at present, that they will judge differently" (Helvidius no. II, August 31, 1793, *Madison Papers*, 15:83; and below, p. 69). Hamilton not only foresaw and expected clashes between the legislative and executive branches; he thought them beneficial. He would argue that these clashes arise not because the president and Congress share executive power as Madison had contended but because they disagree over policy and clash in the exercise of their concurrent authorities (Pacificus no. I, June 29, 1793, *Hamilton Papers*, 15:42; and below, p. 15). Hamilton intimates the possibility or even the likelihood of permanent constitutional clashes over matters of policy which must be settled politically because the Constitution, due to its absence of specificity, simply cannot resolve them. He recognized the essential limitation of law as law in dealing with foreign policy, but Madison did not, at least not in this instance.

In the debate over the president's removal power in the First Congress, Madison had argued that the appointing power was executive in nature, that Senate participation in the appointing power was an exception to the general executive power of the president, and that the president had the exclusive power to remove any officer he appointed by virtue of his general executive power (Removal Power of the President, June 17, 1789, *Madison Papers*, 12:233). But in the debate over neutrality later on, he denied that Senate participation in the treaty-making power constituted a similar exception to the general executive power of the president, and that was because treaty making was more legislative than executive in character: ". . . no analogy, or shade of analogy, can be traced between a power in the supreme officer responsible for the faithful execution of the laws, to displace a subaltern officer employed in the execution of the laws; and a power to make treaties" for "there are sufficient indications that the power of treaties is regarded by the constitution as materially different from mere executive power, and as having more affinity to the legislative than to the executive character" (Helvidius no. I, August 24, 1793, *Madison Papers*, 15:72, 70; and below, pp. 63 and 61). Despite the position Madison had taken in defense of the president's exclusive control over removals in 1789, he now maintained that Senate participation in treaty making extended to interpretation as well as advice and consent.

Madison claimed in the Pacificus-Helvidius debates that Hamilton's reading of executive power introduced "new principles and new constructions" into the Constitution that were intended to remove "the landmarks of power" (Helvidius no. IV, September 14, 1793, *Madison Papers*, 15:107; and below, p. 85). He was, theoretically speaking, a purist, attached to the purity of republican theory, following what he believed to be a fair construction of the Constitution consistent with liberty rather than a liberal construction of executive power. It was the violation of the Constitution issuing from the introduction of "new principles and constructions" into that document that most concerned Madison as well as Jefferson, who saw it as in effect undermining the very sanctity of the constitutional document. Hamilton was arguing that the direction of foreign policy is essentially an executive function, whereas Madison was arguing that the direction of foreign policy is essentially a legislative function by virtue of the Senate's treaty-making and war powers. Hamilton construed the Senate's treaty-making and war powers as exceptions out of the general executive power vested in the president. Although neutrality has since become a congressional prerogative, the Hamiltonian reasoning has established the constitutional basis for the broad exercise of executive powers in foreign affairs, an emphasis which was not at all clear prior to the neutrality debates. In other words, that debate had far wider implications than the neutrality issue itself.

The Neutrality Proclamation represents America's finest hour in the arena of foreign policy. This is highlighted by Hamilton's defense of that proclamation in which the foreign policy powers of the president are elaborated as part of a more complete Constitution, an elaboration which added a dimension that had not previously existed in the original document. The debates clarified certain constitutional principles that we now associate with executive power generally: (1) that the direction of foreign policy is essentially an executive function; (2) that, beyond the enumeration of specific powers in Article II, other powers were deposited in the general grant of executive power in that article; and (3) that the overlapping spheres of power created by the Constitution are necessary for the more effective operation of separation of powers so that the powers themselves can fall within one another's boundaries and at the same time be kept independent of each other.

It can be reasonably inferred from the language of the Constitution that the president receives an undefined, nonenumerated reservoir of power from the clause of Article II containing the general grant of executive power over and above the powers expressed or specifically enumerated in that article. Hamilton sensed that the final structure of the unfinished Constitution might well be determined by the way he would advance his broad construction of certain clauses in that document during his tenure of office, a construction which would give the president a field of action much wider than that outlined by the enumerated powers. Hamilton was not moved to introduce fundamental changes in the Constitution itself, but rather to clarify the necessary and proper role of executive power in foreign affairs. We are sufficiently familiar with written constitutions to know that their essential defect is inflexibility, but whatever defects adhere to what is committed to writing are made up for in part, in the case of our Constitution, by the open-endedness that its leading draftsmen worked into its overall design. We have no difficulty in recognizing therefore that much of the meaning of the Constitution would come through inference or construction. It was apparent that the open-ended character of some of the constitutional provisions afforded opportunities for extending the powers of government beyond their specified limits. Although not given prior sanction by the Constitutional Convention, such additions served to provide a more complete definition of powers without actually changing the ends of government.

ADDENDUM

In the George F. Hopkins edition of 1802, which must be taken as Hamilton's final version of the *Federalist Papers,* he insisted that the edition include his Pacificus. He remarked to Hopkins that "some of his friends had pronounced [it] . . . his best performance," apparently feeling that this was a natural supplement to what he had already written in his commentary on the United States Constitution.

MORTON J. FRISCH

NOTE ON THE TEXT

Hamilton's and Madison's notes are referenced with symbols. The bracketed supplements to these notes include my own additions as well as those retained from the Columbia University Press and University Press of Virginia editions of Hamilton's and Madison's *Papers,* respectively. Bracketed material in the numbered footnotes is mine; unbracketed material is from the Columbia and Virginia editions. Bracketed material within the text itself, i.e., not in footnotes, has been supplied.

THE PACIFICUS-HELVIDIUS DEBATES OF 1793–1794

Washington's Neutrality Proclamation, April 22, 1793

By the President of the
United States of America
A Proclamation

Whereas it appears that a state of war exists between Austria, Prussia, Sardinia, Great Britain, and the United Netherlands, of the one part, and France on the other; and the duty and interest of the United States require, that they should with sincerity and good faith adopt and pursue a conduct friendly and impartial towards the belligerent Powers:

I have therefore thought fit by these presents to declare the disposition of the United States to observe the conduct aforesaid towards those Powers respectively; and to exhort and warn the citizens of the United States carefully to avoid all acts and proceedings whatsoever, which may in any manner tend to contravene such disposition.

And I hereby also make known, that whosoever of the citizens of the United States shall render himself liable to punishment or forfeiture under the law of nations, by committing, aiding, or abetting hostilities against any of the said Powers, or by carrying to any of them those articles which are deemed contraband by the *modern* usage of nations, will not receive the protection of the United States, against such punishment or forfeiture; and further, that I have given instructions to those officers, to whom it belongs, to cause prosecutions to be instituted against all persons, who shall, within the cognizance of the courts of the United States, violate the law of nations, with respect to the Powers at war, or any of them.

Reprinted with permission from *The Papers of Alexander Hamilton*, ed. Harold Syrett et al., vol. 14 (New York: Columbia University Press, 1969), 308–9.

In the following essay, Hamilton attacks the motives of those who opposed President Washington's Neutrality Proclamation of 1793 relative to the war between England and France. It should be read in conjunction with Hamilton's Pacificus essays, which attempt to counter the criticisms of the president's issuance of that proclamation.

Defense of the President's Neutrality Proclamation

[Philadelphia, May 1793]

1. It is a melancholy truth, which every new political occurrence more and more unfolds, that there is a discription of men in this country, irreconcileably adverse to the government of the United States; whose exertions, whatever be the springs of them, whether infatuation or depravity or both, tend to disturb the tranquillity order and prosperity of this now peaceable flourishing and truly happy land. A real and enlightened friend to public felicity cannot observe new confirmations of this fact, without feeling a deep and poignant regret, that human nature should be so refractory and perverse; that amidst a profusion of the bounties and blessings of Providence, political as well as natural, inviting to contentment and gratitude, there should still be found men disposed to cherish and propagate disquietude and alarm; to render suspected and detested the instruments of the felicity, in which they partake; to sacrifice the most substantial advantages, that ever fell to the lot of a people at the shrine of personal envy rivalship and animosity, to the instigations of a turbulent and criminal ambition, or

Reprinted with permission from *The Papers of Alexander Hamilton,* ed. Harold Syrett et al., vol. 14 (New York: Columbia University Press, 1969), 502–7.

to the treacherous phantoms of an ever craving and never to be satisfied spirit of innovation; a spirit, which seems to suggest to its votaries that the most natural and happy state of Society is a state of continual revolution and change—that the welfare of a nation is in exact ratio to the rapidity of the political vicissitudes, which it undergoes—to the frequency and violence of the tempests with which it is agitated.

2.   Yet so the fact unfortunately is—such men there certainly are—and it is essential to our dearest interests to the preservation of peace and good order to the dignity and independence of our public councils—to the real and permanent security of liberty and property—that the Citizens of the UStates should open their eyes to the true characters and designs of the men alluded to—should be upon their guard against their insidious and ruinous machinations.

3.   At this moment a most dangerous combination exists. Those who for some time past have been busy in undermining the constitution and government of the UStates, by indirect attacks, by labouring to render its measures odious, by striving to destroy the confidence of the people in its administration—are now meditating a more direct and destructive war against it—a⟨nd⟩ embodying and arranging their forces and systematising their efforts. Secret clubs are formed and private consultations held. Emissaries are dispatched to distant parts of the United States to effect a concert of views and measures, among the members and partisans of the disorganising corps, in the several states. The language in the confidential circles is that the constitution of the United States is too complex a system—that it savours too much of the pernicious doctrine of "ballances and checks" that it requires to be simplified in its structure, to be purged of some monarchical and aristocratic ingredients which are said to have found their way into it and to be stripped of some dangerous prerogatives, with which it is pretended to be invested.

4.   The noblest passion of the human soul, which no where burns with so pure and bright a flame, as in the breasts of the people of the UStates, is if possible to be made subservient to this fatal project. That zeal for the liberty of mankind, which produced so universal a sympathy in the cause of

3

France in the first stages of its revolution, and which, it is supposed, has not yet yielded to the just reprobation, which a sober temperate and humane people, friends of religion, social order, and justice, enemies to tumult and massacre, to the wanton and lawless shedding of human blood cannot but bestow upon those extravagancies excesses and outrages, which have sullied and which endanger that cause—that laudable, it is not too much to say that holy zeal is intended by every art of misrepresentation and deception to be made the instrument first of controuling finally of overturning the Government of the Union.

5. The ground which has been so wisely taken by the Executive of the UStates, in regard to the present war of Europe against France, is to be the pretext of this mischievous attempt. The people are if possible to be made to believe, that the Proclamation of neutrality issued by the President of the US was unauthorised illegal and officious—inconsistent with the treaties and plighted faith of the Nation—inconsistent with a due sense of gratitude to France for the services rendered us in our late contest for independence and liberty—inconsistent with a due regard for the progress and success of republican principles. Already the presses begin to groan with invective against the Chief Magistrate of the Union, for that prudent and necessary measure; a measure calculated to manifest to the World the pacific position of the Government and to caution the citizens of the UStates against practices, which would tend to involve us in a War the most unequal and calamitous, in which it is possible for a Country to be engaged—a war which would not be unlikely to prove pregnant with still greater dangers and disasters, than that by which we established our existence as an Independent Nation.

6. What is the true solution of this extraordinary appearance? Are the professed the real motives of its authors? They are not. The true object is to disparage in the opinion and affections of his fellow citizens that man who at the head of our armies fought so successfully for the Liberty and Independence, which are now our pride and our boast—who during the war supported the hopes, united the hearts and nerved the arm of his countrymen—who at the close of it, unseduced by ambition & the love of power, soothed

and appeased the discontents of his suffering companions in arms, and with them left the proud scenes of a victorious field for the modest retreats of private life—who could only have been drawn out of these favourite retreats, to aid in the glorious work of ingrafting that liberty, which his sword had contributed to win, upon a stock of which it stood in need and without which it could not flourish—endure—a firm adequate national Government—who at this moment sacrifices his tranquillity and every favourite pursuit to the peremptory call of his country to aid in giving solidity to a fabric, which he has assisted in rearing—whose whole conduct has been one continued proof of his rectitude moderation disinterestedness and patriotism, who whether the evidence of a uniform course of virtuous public actions be considered, or the motives likely to actuate a man placed precisely in his situation be estimated, it may safely be pronounced, can have no other ambition than that of doing good to his Country & transmitting his fame unimpaired to posterity. For what or for whom is he to hazard that rich harvest of glory, which he has acquired that unexampled veneration and love of his fellow Citizens, which he so eminently possesses?

7.   Yet the men alluded to, while they contend with affected zeal for gratitude towards a foreign Nation, which in assisting us was and ought to have been influenced by considerations relative to its own interest—forgetting what is due to a fellow Citizen, who at every hazard rendered essential services to his Country from the most patriotic motives—insidiously endeavour to despoil him of that precious reward of his services, the confidence and approbation of his fellow Citizens.

8.   The present attempt is but the renewal in another form of an attack some time since commenced, and which was only dropped because it was perceived to have excited a general indignation. Domestic arrangements of mere convenience, calculated to reconcile the oeconomy of time with the attentions of decorum and civility were then the topics of malevolent declamation. A more serious article of charge is now opened and seems intended to be urged with greater earnestness and vigour. The merits of it shall be examined in one or two succeeding papers, I trust in a manner, that will evince to every candid mind to futility.

9. To be an able and firm supporter of the Government of the Union is in the eyes of the men referred to a crime sufficient to justify the most malignant persecution. Hence the attacks which have been made and repeated with such persevering industry upon more than one public Character in that Government. Hence the effort which is now going on to depreciate in the eyes and estimation of the People the man whom their unanimous suffrages have placed at the head of it.

10. Hence the pains which are taking to inculcate a discrimination between *principles* and *men* and to represent an attachment to the one as a species of war against the other; an endeavour, which has a tendency to stifle or weaken one of the best and most useful feelings of the human heart—a reverence for merit—and to take away one of the strongest incentives to public virtue—the expectation of public esteem.

11. A solicitude for the character who is attacked forms no part of the motives to this comment. He has deserved too much, and his countrymen are too sensible of it to render any advocation of him necessary. If his virtues and services do not secure his fame and ensure to him the unchangeable attachment of his fellow Citizens, twere in vain to attempt to prop them by anonymous panygeric.

12. The design of the observations which have been made is merely to awaken the public attention to the views of a party engaged in a dangerous conspiracy against the tranquillity and happiness of their country. Aware that their hostile aims against the Government can never succeed til they have subverted the confidence of the people in its present Chief Magistrate, they have at length permitted the suggestions of their enmity to betray them into this hopeless and culpable attempt. If we can destroy his popularity (say they) our work is more than half completed.

13. In proportion as the Citizens of the UStates value the constitution on which their union and happiness depend, in proportion as they tender the blessings of peace and deprecate the calamities of War—ought to be their watchfulness against this success of the artifices which will be employed to endanger that constitution and those blessings. A mortal blow is aimed at both.

14. It imports them infinitely not to be deceived by the protestations which are made—that no harm is meditated against the Constitution—that no design is entertained to involve the peace of the Country. These appearances are necessary to the accomplishment of the plan which has been formed. It is known that the great body of the People are attached to the constitution. It would therefore defeat the intention of destroying it to avow that it exists. It is also known that the People of the UStates are firmly attached to peace. It would consequently frustrate the design of engaging them in the War to tell them that such an object is in contemplation.

15. A more artful course has therefore been adopted. Professions of good will to the Constitution are made without reserve: But every possible art is employed to render the administration and the most zealous and useful friends of the Government odious. The reasoning is obvious. If the people can be persuaded to dislike all the measures of the Government and to dislike all or the greater part of those who have [been] most conspicuous in establishing or conducting it—the passage from this to the dislike and change of the constitution will not be long nor difficult. The abstract idea of regard for a constitution on paper will not long resist a thorough detestation of its practice.

16. In like manner, professions of a disposition to preserve the peace of the Country are liberally made. But the means of effecting the end are condemned; and exertions are used to prejudice the community against them. A proclamation of neutrality in the most cautious form is represented as illegal—contrary to our engagements with and our duty towards one of the belligerent powers. The plain inference is that in the opinion of these characters the UStates are under obligations which do not permit them to be neutral. Of course they are in a situation to become a party in the War from duty.

17. Pains are likewise taken to inflame the zeal of the people for the cause of France and to excite their resentments against the powers at War with her. To what end all this—but to beget if possible a temper in the community which may overrule the moderate or pacific views of the Government.

One of the most controversial opinions of Hamilton's political career was his justification of executive independence in foreign policy questions in the debate over Washington's Neutrality Proclamation. Hamilton argues in the following essay that the president's power to make such a proclamation issues from the general grant of executive power, which includes conducting foreign relations; from the president's primary responsibility in the formation of treaties; and from the power of the execution of the laws, of which treaties form a part.

Pacificus Number I

[Philadelphia, June 29, 1793]

As attempts are making very dangerous to the peace, and it is to be feared not very friendly to the constitution of the UStates—it becomes the duty of those who wish well to both to endeavour to prevent their success.

The objections which have been raised against the Proclamation of Neutrality lately issued by the President have been urged in a spirit of acrimony and invective, which demonstrates, that more was in view than merely a free discussion of an important public measure; that the discussion covers a design of weakening the confidence of the People in the author of the measure; in order to remove or lessen a powerful obstacle to the success of an opposition to the Government, which however it may change its form, according to circumstances, seems still to be adhered to and pursued with persevering Industry.

This Reflection adds to the motives connected with the measure itself to recommend endeavours by proper explanations to place it in a just light.

Reprinted with permission from *The Papers of Alexander Hamilton,* ed. Harold Syrett et al., vol. 15 (New York: Columbia University Press, 1969), 33–43.

Such explanations at least cannot but be satisfactory to those who may not have leisure or opportunity for pursuing themselves an investigation of the subject, and who may wish to perceive that the policy of the Government is not inconsistent with its obligations or its honor.

The objections in question fall under three heads—

1. That the Proclamation was without authority

2. That it was contrary to our treaties with France

3. That it was contrary to the gratitude, which is due from this to that country; for the succours rendered us in our own Revolution.

4. That it was out of time & unnecessary.

In order to judge of the solidity of the first of these objection[s], it is necessary to examine what is the nature and design of a proclamation of neutrality.

The true nature & design of such an act is—to *make known* to the powers at War and to the Citizens of the Country, whose Government does the Act that such country is in the condition of a Nation at Peace with the belligerent parties, and under no obligations of Treaty, to become an *associate in the war* with either of them; that this being its situation its intention is to observe a conduct conformable with it and to perform towards each the duties of neutrality; and as a consequence of this state of things, to give warning to all within its jurisdiction to abstain from acts that shall contravene those duties, under the penalties which the laws of the land (of which the law of Nations is a part) annexes to acts of contravention.

This, and no more, is conceived to be the true import of a Proclamation of Neutrality.

It does not imply, that the Nation which makes the declaration will forbear to perform to any of the warring Powers any stipulations in Treaties which can be performed without rendering it an *associate* or *party* in the War. It therefore does not imply in our case, that the UStates will not make those distinctions, between the present belligerent powers, which are stipulated in the 17th and 22d articles of our Treaty with France; because these distinctions are not incompatible with a state of neutrality; they will in no shape render the UStates an *associate* or *party* in the War. This must be evident, when it is considered, that even to furnish *determinate* succours, of a certain number of Ships or troops, to a Power at War, in consequence of *antecedent treaties having no particular reference to the existing war,* is not inconsistent with neutrality; a position well established by the doctrines of Writers and the practice of Nations.*

But no special aids, succours or favors having relation to war, not positively and precisely stipulated by some Treaty of the above description, can be afforded to either party, without a breach of neutrality.

In stating that the Proclamation of Neutrality does not imply the non performance of any stipulations of Treaties which are not of a nature to make the Nation an associate or party in the war, it is conceded that an execution of the clause of Guarantee contained in the 11th article of our Treaty of Alliance with France would be contrary to the sense and spirit of the Proclamation; because it would engage us with our whole force as an *associate* or *auxiliary* in the War; it would be much more than the case of a definite limited succour, previously ascertained.

It follows that the Proclamation is virtually a manifestation of the sense of the Government that the UStates are, *under the circumstances of the case, not bound* to execute the clause of Guarantee.

If this be a just view of the true force and import of the Proclamation, it will remain to see whether the President in issuing it acted within his proper sphere, or stepped beyond the bounds of his constitutional authority and duty.

It will not be disputed that the management of the affairs of this country with foreign nations is confided to the Government of the UStates.

It can as little be disputed, that a Proclamation of Neutrality, where a Nation is at liberty to keep out of a War in which other Nations are engaged and means so to do, is a *usual* and a *proper* measure. *Its main object and effect are to prevent the Nation being immediately responsible for acts done by its citizens, without the privity or connivance of the Government, in contravention of the principles of neutrality.*†

---

* See Vatel, Book III, Chap. VI, § 101 [Vattel, *Law of Nations*].
† See Vatel, Book III, Chap. VII, § 113.

An object this of the greatest importance to a Country whose true interest lies in the preservation of peace.

The inquiry then is—what department of the Government of the UStates is the prop⟨er⟩ one to make a declaration of Neutrality in the cases in which the engagements ⟨of⟩ the Nation permit and its interests require such a declaration.

A correct and well informed mind will discern at once that it can belong neit⟨her⟩ to the Legislative nor Judicial Department and of course must belong to the Executive.

The Legislative Department is not the *organ* of intercourse between the UStates and foreign Nations. It is charged neither with *making* nor *interpreting* Treaties. It is therefore not naturally that Organ of the Government which is to pronounce the existing condition of the Nation, with regard to foreign Powers, or to admonish the Citizens of their obligations and duties as founded upon that condition of things. Still less is it charged with enforcing the execution and observance of these obligations and those duties.

It is equally obvious that the act in question is foreign to the Judiciary Department of the Government. The province of that Department is to decide litigations in particular cases. It is indeed charged with the interpretation of treaties; but it exercises this function only in the litigated cases; that is where contending parties bring before it a specific controversy. It has no concern with pronouncing upon the external political relations of Treaties between Government and Government. This position is too plain to need being insisted upon.

It must then of necessity belong to the Executive Department to exercise the function in Question—when a proper case for the exercise of it occurs.

It appears to be connected with that department in various capacities, as the *organ* of intercourse between the Nation and foreign Nations—as the interpreter of the National Treaties in those cases in which the Judiciary is not competent, that is in the cases between Government and Government—as that Power, which is charged with the Execution of the Laws, of which Treaties form a part—as that Power which is charged with the command and application of the Public Force.

This view of the subject is so natural and obvious—so analogous to general theory and practice—that no doubt can be entertained of its justness, unless such doubt can be deduced from particular provisions of the Constitution of the UStates.

Let us see then if cause for such doubt is to be found in that constitution.

The second Article of the Constitution of the UStates, section 1st, establishes this general Proposition, That "The EXECUTIVE POWER shall be vested in a President of the United States of America."

The same article in a succeeding Section proceeds to designate particular cases of Executive Power. It declares among other things that the President shall be Commander in Cheif of the army and navy of the UStates and of the Militia of the several states when called into the actual service of the UStates, that he shall have power by and with the advice of the senate to make treaties; that it shall be his duty to receive ambassadors and other public Ministers and to take care that the laws be faithfully executed.

It would not consist with the rules of sound construction to consider this enumeration of particular authorities as derogating from the more comprehensive grant contained in the general clause, further than as it may be coupled with express restrictions or qualifications; as in regard to the cooperation of the Senate in the appointment of Officers and the making of treaties; which are qualifica⟨tions⟩ of the general executive powers of appointing officers and making treaties: Because the difficulty of a complete and perfect specification of all the cases of Executive authority would naturally dictate the use of general terms—and would render it improbable that a specification of certain particulars was designd as a substitute for those terms, when antecedently used. The different mode of expression employed in the constitution in regard to the two powers the Legislative and the Executive serves to confirm this inference. In the article which grants the legislative powers of the Governt. the expressions are—"*All Legislative powers herein granted shall be vested in a Congress of the UStates*"; in that which grants the Executive Power the expressions are, as already quoted "The EXECUTIVE Po⟨WER⟩ shall be vested in a President of the UStates of America."

The enumeration ought rather therefore to be considered as intended by way of greater caution, to specify and regulate the principal articles implied in the definition of Executive Power; leaving the rest to flow from the general grant of that power, interpreted in conformity to other parts ⟨of⟩ the constitution and to the principles of free government.

The general doctrine then of our constitution is, that the EXECUTIVE POWER of the Nation is vested in the President; subject only to the *exceptions* and *qu[a]lifications* which are expressed in the instrument.

Two of these have been already noticed—the participation of the Senate in the appointment of Officers and the making of Treaties. A third remains to be mentioned the right of the Legislature "to declare war and grant letters of marque and reprisal."

With these exceptions the EXECUTIVE POWER of the Union is completely lodged in the President. This mode of construing the Constitution has indeed been recognized by Congress in formal acts, upon full consideration and debate. The power of removal from office is an important instance.

And since upon general principles for reasons already given, the issuing of a proclamation of neutrality is merely an Executive Act; since also the general Executive Power of the Union is vested in the President, the conclusion is, that the step, which has been taken by him, is liable to no just exception on the score of authority.

It may be observed that this Inference w⟨ould⟩ be just if the power of declaring war had ⟨not⟩ been vested in the Legislature, but that ⟨this⟩ power naturally includes the right of judg⟨ing⟩ whether the Nation is under obligations to m⟨ake⟩ war or not.

The answer to this is, that however true it may be, that th⟨e⟩ right of the Legislature to declare wa⟨r⟩ includes the right of judging whether the N⟨ation⟩ be under obligations to make War or not—it will not follow that the Executive is in any case excluded from a similar right of Judgment, in the execution of its own functions.

If the Legislature have a right to make war on the one hand—it is on the other the duty of the Executive to preserve Peace till war is declared;

and in fulfilling that duty, it must necessarily possess a right of judging what is the nature of the obligations which the treaties of the Country impose on the Government; and when in pursuance of this right it has concluded that there is nothing in them inconsistent with a *state* of neutrality, it becomes both its province and its duty to enforce the laws incident to that state of the Nation. The Executive is charged with the execution of all laws, the laws of Nations as well as the Municipal law, which recognises and adopts those laws. It is consequently bound, by faithfully executing the laws of neutrality, when that is the state of the Nation, to avoid giving a cause of war to foreign Powers.

This is the direct and proper end of the proclamation of neutrality. It declares to the UStates their situation with regard to the Powers at war and makes known to the Community that the laws incident to that situation will be enforced. In doing this, it conforms to an established usage of Nations, the operation of which as before remarked is to obviate a responsibility on the part of the whole Society, for secret and unknown violations of the rights of any of the warring parties by its citizens.

Those who object to the proclamation will readily admit that it is the right and duty of the Executive to judge of, or to interpret, those articles of our treaties which give to France particular privileges, in order to the enforcement of those privileges: But the necessary consequence of this is, that the Executive must judge what are the proper bounds of those privileges—what rights are given to other nations by our treaties with them—what rights the law of Nature and Nations gives and our treaties permit, in respect to those Nations with whom we have no treaties; in fine what are the reciprocal rights and obligations of the United States & of all & each of the powers at War.

The right of the Executive to receive ambassadors and other public Ministers may serve to illustrate the relative duties of the Executive and Legislative Departments. This right includes that of judging, in the case of a Revolution of Government in a foreign Country, whether the new rulers are competent organs of the National Will and ought to ⟨be⟩ recognised or not: And where a treaty antecedently exists between the UStates and such nation that right involves the power of giving operation or not to such treaty. For until the new Government is *acknowleged,* the treaties between the nations, as far at least as regards *public* rights, are of course suspended.

This power of determ[in]ing virtually in the case supposed upon the operation of national Treaties as a consequence, of the power to receive ambassadors and other public Ministers, is an important instance of the right of the Executive to decide the obligations of the Nation with regard to foreign Nations. To apply it to the case of France, if the⟨re⟩ had been a Treaty of alliance *offensive* ⟨and⟩ defensive between the UStates and that Coun⟨try,⟩ the unqualified acknowlegement of the new Government would have put the UStates in a condition to become an associate in the War in which France was engaged—and would have laid the Legislature under an obligation, if required, and there was otherwise no valid excuse, of exercising its power of declaring war.

This serves as an example of the right of the Executive, in certain cases, to determine the condition of the Nation, though it may consequentially affect the proper or improper exercise of the Power of the Legislature to declare war. The Executive indeed cannot control the exercise of that power—further than by the exer[c]ise of its general right of objecting to all acts of the Legislature; liable to being overruled by two thirds of both houses of Congress. The Legislature is free to perform its own duties according to its own sense of them—though the Executive in the exercise of its constitutional powers, may establish an antecedent state of things which ought to weigh in the legislative decisions. From the division of the Executive Power there results, in referrence to it, a *concurrent* authority, in the distributed cases.

Hence in the case stated, though treaties can only be made by the President and Senate, their activity may be continued or suspended by the President alone.

No objection has been made to the Presidents having acknowleged the Republic of France, by the Reception of its Minister, without having consulted the Senate; though that body is connected with him in the making of Treaties, and though the consequence of his act of reception is to give operation to the Treaties heretofore made with that Country: But he is censured for having declared the UStates to be in a state of peace & neutrality, with regard to the Powers at War; because the right of *changing* that state & *declaring war* belongs to the Legislature.

It deserves to be remarked, that as the participation of the senate in the making of Treaties and the power of the Legislature to declare war are exceptions out of the general "Executive Power" vested in the President, they are to be construed strictly—and ought to be extended no further than is essential to their execution.

While therefore the Legislature can alone declare war, can alone actually transfer the nation from a state of Peace to a state of War—it belongs to the "Executive Power," to do whatever else the laws of Nations cooperating with the Treaties of the Country enjoin, in the intercourse of the UStates with foreign Powers.

In this distribution of powers the wisdom of our constitution is manifested. It is the province and duty of the Executive to preserve to the Nation the blessings of peace. The Legislature alone can interrupt those blessings, by placing the Nation in a state of War.

But though it has been thought adviseable to vindicate the authority of the Executive on this broad and comprehensive ground—it was not absolutely necessary to do so. That clause of the constitution which makes it his duty to "take care that the laws be faithfully executed" might alone have been relied upon, and this simple process of argument pursued.

The President is the constitutional EXECUTOR of the laws. Our Treaties and the laws of Nations form a part of the law of the land. He who is to execute the laws must first judge for himself of their meaning. In order to the observance of that conduct, which the laws of nations combined with our treaties prescribed to this country, in reference to the present War in Europe, it was necessary for the President to judge for himself whether there was any thing in our treaties incompatible with an adherence to neutrality. Having judged that there was not, he had a right, and if in his opinion the interests of the Nation required it, it was his duty, as Executor of the laws, to proclaim the neutrality of the Nation, to exhort all persons to observe it, and to warn them of the penalties which would attend its non observance.

The Proclamation has been represented as enacting some new law. This is a view of it entirely erroneous. It only proclaims a *fact* with regard to the *existing state* of the Nation, informs the citizens of what the laws previously established require of them in that state, & warns them that these laws will be put in execution against the Infractors of them.

Hamilton argues that the 1778 treaty with France was a defensive alliance and that the war France has now undertaken was not forced on her by an attack of some third power. France is now fighting an offensive war and therefore America's involvement is not required under the terms of the treaty.

Pacificus Number II

[Philadelphia, July 3, 1793]

The second & principal objection to the Proclamation namely that it is inconsistent with the Treaties between the United States and France will now be examined.

It has been already shewn, that it is not inconsistent with the performance of any of the stipulations in those Treaties, which would not make us an associate or party in the war and particularly, that it is compatible with the privileges secured to France by the 17 & 22d articles of the Treaty of Commerce; which, except the clause of Guarantee, constitute the most material discriminations to be found in our treaties in favour of that Country.

Official documents have likewise appeared, in the public papers, which are understood to be authentic, that serve as a comment upon the sense of the proclamation in this particular; proving that it was not deemed by the Executive incompatible with the performance of the stipulations in those articles, and that in practice they are intended to be observed.

It has however been admitted, that the declaration of neutrality excludes the idea of an execution of the clause of Guarantee.

Reprinted with permission from *The Papers of Alexander Hamilton*, ed. Harold Syrett et al., vol. 15 (New York: Columbia University Press, 1969), 55–63.

It becomes necessary therefore to examine whether the United States would have a valid justification for not complying with it, in case of their being called upon for that purpose by France.

Without knowing how far the reasons, which have occurred to me, may have influenced the President, there appear to me to exist very good and substantial grounds for a refusal.

The Alliance between the United States and France is a *Defensive Alliance*. In the Caption of it it is denominated a "Treaty of Alliance eventual and *defensive*." In the body of it, (Article the 2) it is again called a *defensive Alliance*. The words of that Article are as follow "The essential and direct end of the present *Defensive Alliance* is to maintain effectually the liberty, sovereignty, and independence absolute and unlimited, of the United States, as well in matters of government as of commerce."

The predominant quality or character then of our alliance with France is that it is *defensive* in its principle. Of course, the meaning obligation and force of every stipulation in the Treaty must be tested and determined by that principle. It is not necessary (and would be absurd) that it should be repeated in every article. It is sufficient that it be once declared, to be understood in every part of the Treaty, unless coupled with express negative words excludi⟨ng⟩ the implication.

The great question consequently is—What are the nature and effect of a defensive alliance? When does the *casus foederis*, or *condition* of the contract take place, in such an alliance?

Reason the concurring opinions of Writers and the practice of Nations will answer—"When either of the allies is *attacked*, when war is made upon him not when he makes war upon another." In other words, The stipulated assistance is to be given to the ally, when engaged in a *defensive* not when engaged in an *offensive* war. This obligation to assist only in a defensive war constitutes the essential difference between a defensive alliance and one which is both offensive and defensive. In the latter case there is an obligation to cooperate as well when the war on the part of our ally is offensive as when it is defensive. To affirm therefore that the UStates are bound to assist France in the War in which she is at present engaged would be to convert our Treaty with her into an Alliance Offensive and Defensive contrary to the express & reiterated declarations of the Instrument itself.

This assertion implies that the War in question is an *offensive war* on the part of France.

And so it undoubtedly is with regard to all the powers with whom she was at War at the time of issuing the Proclamation.

No position is better established than that the Power which *first declares* or *actually begins* a WAR, whatever may have been the causes leading to it, is that which makes an *offensive war.* Nor is there any doubt that France first declared and began the War against Austria, Prussia, Savoy Holland England and Spain.

Upon this point there is apt to be some incorrectness of ideas. Those, who have not examined subjects of such a Nature are led to imagine that the party which commits the first injury or gives the first provocation is on the offensive side in the war, though begun by the other party.

But the cause or occasion of the War and the War itself are things entirely distinct. Tis the commencement of the War itself that decides the question of being on the offensive or defensive. All writers on the laws of Nations agree in this principle but it is more accurately laid down in the following extract from BURLAMAQUI.*

"Neither are we to believe (says he) that he *who first injures* another begins by that an *offensive* War and that the other *who demands the satisfaction for the Injury received* is *always* on the *Defensive.* There are a great many *unjust acts which may kindle a War* and which however are not the war itself, as the ill treatment of a Princes Ambassador the plundering of his subjects &c."

"If therefore we take up arms to revenge such an unjust act we commence an *offensive* but a just war; and the Prince who has done the injury and will not give satisfaction makes a *defensive* but an unjust war."

---

*Vol. II, Book IV, Chap. III, Sections IV & V [Burlamaqui, *Principles of Political Law*].

"We must therefore affirm, in general, that the first who takes up arms whether *justly* or *unjustly* commences an *offensive* War & he who opposes him whether with or without reason, begins a defensive War."

France then being on the *offensive* in the war, in which she is engaged, and our alliance with her being *defensive* only, it follows that the *casus foederis* or condition of our guarantee cannot take place; and that the UStates are free to refuse a performance of that guarantee, if demanded.

Those who are disposed to justify indiscriminately every thing, in the conduct of France, may reply that though the war in point of form may be offensive on her part, yet in point of principle it is defensive—was in each instance a mere anticipation of attacks meditated against her, and was justified by previous aggressions of the opposite parties.

It is believed that it would be a sufficient answer to this observation to say that in determ[in]ing the *legal* and *positive* obligations of the UStates the only point of inquiry is—whether the War was *in fact* begun by France or by her enemies; that All beyond this would be too vague, too liable to dispute, too much matter of opinion to be a proper criterion of National Conduct; that when a war breaks out between two Nations, all other nations, in regard to the positive rights of the parties and their positive duties towards them are bound to consider it as equally just on both sides   that consequently in a *defensive* alliance, when *war is made upon* one of the allies, the other is bound to fulfil the conditions stipulated on its part, without inquiry whether the war is rightfully begun or not—as on the other hand when war is begun by one of the allies the other is exempted from the obligation of assisting; however just the commencement of it may have been.

The foundation of this doctrine, is the utility of clear and certain rules for determining the reciprocal duties of nations—that as little as possible may be left to opinion and the subterfuges of a refining or unfaithful casuistry.

Some writers indeed of great authority affirm that it is a tacit condition of every Treaty of alliance, that one ally is not bound to assist the other in a war manifestly unjust. But this is questioned on the ground which has been stated by other respectable authorities. And though the manifest injustice of the war has been affirmed by some, to be a good cause for not executing the formal obligations of a treaty, I have no where found it maintained, that the justice of a war is a consideration, which can *oblige* a nation to do what its formal obligations do not require; as in the case of a *defensive* alliance, to furnish the succours stipulated, though the formal obligation did not exist, by reason of the ally having begun the war, instead of being the party attacked.

But if this were not the true doctrine, an impartial examination would prove, that with respect to some of the powers, France is not blameless in the circumstances, which preceded and led to the war with those powers; that if she received, she also gave cause of offense, and that the justice of the War on her side is, in those cases, not a little problematical.

There are prudential reasons which dissuade from going largely into this examination; unless it shall be rendered necessary by the future turn of the discussion.

It will be sufficient here, to notice cursorily the following facts.

France committed an aggression upon Holland in declaring free the navigation of the Scheldt and acting upon that declaration; contrary to Treaties in which she had explicitly acknowleged and even guaranteed the exclusive right of Holland to the navigation of that River and contrary to the doctrines of the best Writers and established usages of Nations, in such cases.

She gave a general and just cause of alarm to Nations, by that Decree of the 19th. of November 1792 whereby the Convention, in the name of the French Nation, declare that they will grant *fraternity* and *assistance* to every People who *wish* to recover their liberty and charge the Executive Power to send the necessary orders to *the Generals* to give assistance to such people, and to *defend those citizens who may have been or who may be vexed for the cause of liberty;* which decree was ordered to be printed *in all languages.*

When a Nation has actually come to a resolution to throw off a yoke, under which it may have groaned, and to assert its liberties—it is justifiable and meritorious in another nation to afford assistance to the one which has been oppressed & is *in the act* of liberating itself; but it is not warrantable for any Nation *beforehand* to hold out a general invitation to insurrection and revolution, by promising to assist *every people* who may *wish* to recover their liberty and to defend *those citizens,* of every country, *who may have been or who may be vexed for the cause of liberty;* still less to commit to the GENERALS of its armies the discretionary power of judging when the Citizens of a foreign Country have been vexed for the cause of Liberty by their own government.

The latter part of the decree amounted exactly to what France herself has most complained of—an interference by one nation in the internal Government of another.

Vatel justly observes, as a consequence of the Liberty & Independence of Nations—"That it does not belong to any foreign Power to take cognizance of the administration of the *sovereign* of another country, to set himself up as a judge of his Conduct or to oblige him to alter it."[1]

Such a conduct as that indicated by this Decree has a natural tendency to disturb the tranquillity of nations, to excite fermentation and revolt every where; and therefore justified neutral powers, who were in a situation to be affected by it in taking measures to repress the spirit by which it had been dictated.

But the principle of this Decree received a more particular application to Great Britain by some subsequent circumstances.

Among the proofs of this are two answers, which were given by the President of the National Convention at a public sitting on the 28th. of November to two different addresses; one presented by a Deputation from "The Society for constitutional information in London" the other by a deputation of English & Irish Citizens at Paris.

The following are extracts from these answers.

"The shades of Penn, of *Hambden* and of *Sydney* hover over your heads; and *the moment without doubt approaches, in which the French will bring congratulations to the National Convention of Great Britain.*"

"Nature and *principles* draw *towards us* England Scotland and Ireland. Let the cries of friendship resound through the two REPUBLICS." "Principles

---

1. Vattel, *Law of Nations,* I, 138.

are waging war against Tyranny, which will fall under the blows of philoso-phy. *Royalty in Europe is either destroyed or on the point of perishing,* on the ruins of feudality; and the *Declaration of Rights placed by the side of thrones is a devouring fire which will consume them.* WORTHY REPUBLICANS &c."

Declarations of this sort cannot but be considered as a direct applica-tion of the principle of the Decree to Great Britain; as an open patronage of a Revolution in that Country; a conduct which proceeding from the head of the body that governed France in the presence and on behalf of that body was unquestionably an offense and injury to the Nation to which it related.

The decree of the 15 of November is another cause of offence to all the Governments of Europe. By That Decree *"The French Nation declares,* that it will *treat as enemies the people,* who *refusing* or *renouncing* liberty and equal-ity *are desirous* of preserving their *Prince* and *privileged casts*— or of *entering into an accomodation* with them &c." This decree was little short of a decla-ration of War against all Nations, having *princes* and *privileged classes.*

The *incorporation* of the territories, over which the arms of France had temporarily prevailed, *with* and *as a part* of herself is another violation of the rights of Nations into which the Convention was betrayed by an intem-perate zeal, if not by a culpable ambition.

The laws of Nations give to a Power at War nothing more than a usu-fructuary or possessory right to the territories, which it conquers; suspend-ing the absolute dominion & property till a treaty of Peace or something equivalent shall cede or relinquish the conquered territory to the Conqueror. This principle is one of the greatest importance to the tranquillity and se-curity of Nations; facilitating an adjustment of the quarrels and the preser-vation of ancient limits.

But France, by incorporating with herself, in several instances, the ter-ritories she had acquired, violated this important principle and multiplied indefinitely the obstacles to peace and accommodation. The Doctrine, *that a Nation cannot consent to its own dismemberment, but in a case of extreme ne-cessity,* immediately attached itself to all the incorporated territories. While the progressive augmentation of the dominions of the most powerful nation in Europe, on a principle not of temporary acquisition, but of permanent union, threatened the independence of all other countries and give to neighbouring neutral powers the justest cause of umbrage and alarm.

It is a principle well agreed & founded on the best reasons, that whenever a particular nation adopts maxims of conduct contrary to ⟨th⟩ose generally established among nations calculated to disturb their tranquillity & to expose their safety, they may justifiably make a common cause to oppose & controul such Nation.

Whatever partial[it]y may be entertained for the general object of the French Revolution, it is impossible for any well informed or soberminded man not to condemn the proceedings which have been stated; as repugnant to the general rights of Nations, to the true principles of liberty, to the freedom of opinion of mankind; & not to acknowlege as a consequence of this, that the justice of the war on the part of France, with regard to some of the powers with which she is engaged, is from those causes questionable enough to free the UStates from all embarrassment on that score; if it be at all incumbent upon them to go into the inquiry.

The policy of a defensive alliance is so essentially distinct from that of an offensive one, that it is every way important not to confound their effects. The first kind has in view the prudent object of mutual defence, when either of the allies is involuntarily forced into a war by the attack by some third power. The latter kind subjects the peace of each ally to the will of the other, and obliges each to partake in the wars of policy & interest, as well as in those of safety and defence, of the other. To preserve their boundaries distinct it is necessary that each kind should be governed by plain and obvious rules. This would not be the case, if instead of taking the simple fact of who begun the war as a guide, it was necessary to travel into metaphysical niceties about the justice or injustice of the cause which led to it. Since also the not furnishing a stipulated succour, when it is due, is itself a cause of War, it is very requisite, that there should be some palpable criterion for ascertaining *when it is due*. This criterion as before observed, in a defensive alliance is the *commencement* or not of the war by our ally, as a mere matter of fact.

Other topics calculated to illustrate the position, that the UStates are not bound to execute the clause of guarantee; are reserved for another paper.

Hamilton is attempting to show why it would not be in the national interest to engage in a war with France against England and the European powers on the grounds that self-preservation is the first duty of a nation. American involvement in a war that placed the maritime forces of all Europe against her could lead to the entire destruction of her trade.

Pacificus Number III

[Philadelphia, July 6, 1793]

France at the time of issuing the proclamation was engaged & likely to be engaged in war, with all or almost all Europe; without a single ally in that quarter of the Globe.

In such a state of things, it is evident, that however she may be able to defend herself at home (a thing probably still practicable if her factions can be appeased, and system and order introduced) she cannot make any *external* efforts, in any degree proportioned to those which can be made against her.

By this situation of things alone, the UStates would be dispensed from an obligation to embark in her quarrel.

It is known that we are wholly destitute of naval force. France, with all the great maritime Powers united against her, is unable to supply this deficiency. She can not afford us that species of cooperation, which is necessary to render our efforts useful to her and to prevent our experiencing the intire destruction of our Trade and the most calamitous inconveniences in other respects.

Reprinted with permission from *The Papers of Alexander Hamilton*, ed. Harold Syrett et al., vol. 15 (New York: Columbia University Press, 1969), 65–69.

Our guarantee does not respect France herself. It does not relate to her own immediate defence or preservation. It relates merely to the defence & preservation of her American colonies; objects of which (though of considerable importance) she might be deprived and yet remain a great and powerful and a happy Nation.

In the actual situation of this Country, and in relation to an object so secondary to France, it may fairly be maintained, that an ability in her to supply in a competent degree our deficiency of naval force is a *condition* of our obligation to perform the Guarantee on our part.

Had the United States a powerful marine or could they command one in time, this reasoning would not be solid; but circumstanced as they are, it is presumed to be well founded.

There would be no proportion between the mischiefs and perils, to which the UStates would expose themselves by embarking in the War, and the benefit *which the nature of their stipulation aims at securing* to France, or that, which it would be in their power actually to render her, by becoming a party.

This disproportion would be a valid reason for not executing the Guarantee. All contracts are to receive a reasonable construction. Self preservation is the first duty of a Nation; and though in the performance of stipulations relating to war, good faith requires that the *ordinary hazards* of war should be fairly encountered, because they are directly contemplated by such stipulations, yet it does not require that *extraordinary* and *extreme* hazards should be run; especially where the object, for which they are to be run, is only a *partial* and *particular* interest of the ally, for whom they are to be run.

As in the present instance good faith does not require, that the UStates should put in jeopardy their essent⟨ial⟩ interests, perhaps their very existence, in one of the most unequal contests, in which a nation could be engaged—to secure to France what?—her West India Islands and other less important possessions in America. For it is to be remembered, that the stipulations of the UStates do in no event reach beyond this point. If they were upon the strength of their Guarantee, to engage in the War, and could make any arrangement with the Belligerent Powers, for securing to

France those Islands and those possessions, they would be at perfect liberty instantly to withdraw. They would not be bound to prosecute the War one moment longer.

They are under no obligation, in any event, as far as the faith of treaties is concerned; to assist France in the defence of her liberty; a topic on which so much has been said, so very little to the purpose as it regards the present question.

The Contest in which the UStates would plunge themselves, were they to take part with France, would possibly be still more unequal, than that in which France herself is engaged. With the possessions of Great Britain and Spain on both Flanks, the numerous Indian tribes, under the influence and direction of those Powers, along our whole Interior frontier, with a long extended sea coast—with no maritime force of our own, and with the maritime force of all Europe against us, with no fortifications whatever and with a population not exceeding four Millions—it is impossible to imagine a more unequal contest, than that in which we should be involved in the case supposed; a contest from which, we are dissuaded by the most cogent motives of self preservation, as well as of Interest.

We may learn from Vatel one of the best Writers on the laws of Nations that "If a State which has promised succours finds itself unable to furnish them, its very inability is its exemption; and if the furnishing the succours would expose it to an *evident* danger this also is a lawful dispensation. The case would render the Treaty *pernicious* to the state and *therefore not obligatory*. But this applies to an *imminent danger* threatening the *safety* of the State; *the case of such a danger is tacitly and necessarily reserved in every Treaty.*"*

If too (as no sensible and candid man will deny) the extent of the present combination against France is in a degree to be ascribed to imprudences on her part—the *exemption* to the UStates is still more manifest and complete. No country is bound to partake in hazards of the most critical kind, which may have been produced or promoted, by the Indiscretion and

---

*See Book III, Chap. VI, § 92 [Vattel, *Law of Nations*, II, 32].

intemperance of another. This is an obvious dictate of reason, with which the common sense and common Practice of Mankind coincide.

To the foregoing considerations it may perhaps be added, with no small degree of force, that military stipulations in national Treaties contemplate only the *ordinary* case of *foreign war,* and are irrelative to the contests which grow out of REVOLUTIONS OF GOVERNMENT; unless where they have express reference to a Revolution begun, or where there is a guarantee of the existing constitution of a nation, or where there is a *personal* alliance for the defence of a prince and his family.*

The Revolution in France is the primitive source of the War, in which she is engaged. The restoration of the monarchy is the avowed object of some of her enemies—and the implied one of all of them. That question then is essentially involved in the principle of the war; a question certainly never in the contemplation of that Government, with which our Treaty was made, and it may thence be fairly inferred never intended to be embraced by it.

The inference would be that the UStates have fulfilled the utmost that could be claimed by the Nation of France, when they so far respected its decision as to recognise the newly constituted Powers; giving operation to the Treaty of Alliance for *future occasions, but considering the present war as a tacit exception.* Perhaps too this exception is in other respects due to the circumstances under which the engagements between the two Countries were contracted. It is impossible, prejudice apart, not to perceive a delicate embarrassment ⟨bet⟩ween the *theory* and *fact* of ⟨our political relations⟩ to France.

On these grounds, also, as ⟨well⟩ as on that of the present War being *of* ⟨ *fensive* ⟩ on the side of France—The USta⟨tes have⟩ valid and honorable pleas to offer ⟨against⟩ the Execution of the Guarantee, ⟨if⟩ it should be claimed of them by France. And the President was in every view fully justified in pronouncing, that the duty and interest of the UStates dictated a Neutrality in the War.

*Puffendorf, Book VIII, Chap. IX, Section IX [Pufendorf, *Of the Law of Nature and Nations*].

Washington's Neutrality Proclamation had the effect of annulling the eleventh article of America's 1778 Treaty of Alliance with France. One of the arguments made in opposition to the proclamation was that it was inconsistent with the gratitude due to France for assistance to America during its war with England. Hamilton maintains in the following essay that mutual interest and reciprocal advantage are much sounder bases for relations among nations than gratitude. This is an important statement because it appears to call for concentration less on moralism than on the realities of power. Hamilton confronts the doctrine that individual morality should be the standard for international conduct with the demand for the preservation of the state. He asserts that the rule of morality is not the same between nations as between individuals, but not that political life is less moral than private life. What he suggests is that political life, generally speaking, is more moral than private life in that it offers a greater opportunity for moral action. That moral action is directed toward collective rather than individual conduct.

Pacificus Number IV

[Philadelphia, July 10, 1793]

A third objection to the Proclamation is, that it is inconsistent with the gratitude due to France, for the services rendered us in our own Revolution.

Those who make this objection disavow at the same time all intention to advocate the position that the United States *ought to take part in the War.* They profess to be friends to our remaining at Peace. What then do they mean by the objection?

Reprinted with permission from *The Papers of Alexander Hamilton,* ed. Harold Syrett et al., vol. 15 (New York: Columbia University Press, 1969), 82–86.

If it be no breach of gratitude to refrain from joining France in the War—how can it be a breach of gratitude to declare that such is our disposition and intention?

The two positions are at variance with each other; and the true inference is either that those who make the objection really wish to engage this country in the war, or that they seek a pretext for censuring the conduct of the chief Magistrate, for some purpose, very different from the public good.

They endeavour in vain to elude this inference by saying, that the Proclamation places France upon an *equal* footing with her enemies; while our Treaties require distinctions in her favour, and our relative situation would dictate kind offices to her, which ought not to be granted to her adversaries.

They are not ignorant, that the Proclamation is reconcileable with both those objects, as far as they have any foundation in truth or propriety.

It has been shewn, that the promise of "a *friendly* and *impartial* conduct" towards all the belligerent powers is not inconsistent with the performance of any stipulations in our treaties, which would not include our becoming an associate in the Wars; and it has been observed, that the conduct of the Executive, in regard to the 17th and 22 articles of the Treaty of Commerce, is an unequivocal comment upon those terms. The expressions indeed were naturally to be understood with the exception of those matters of positive compact, which would not amount to taking part in the War; for a nation then observes a friendly and impartial conduct, towards two powers at war—when it only performs to one of them what it is obliged to do by the positive stipulations of antecedent treaties; those stipulations not amounting to a participation in the war.

Neither do those expressions imply, that the UStates will not exercise their discretion, in doing kind offices to some of the parties, without extending them to the others; *so long as those offices have no relation to war:* For kind offices of that description may, consistently with neutrality, be shewn to one party and refused to another.

If the objectors mean that the UStates ought to favour France, *in thin⟨gs relating⟩ to war and where they are not bound ⟨to do it⟩ by Treaty*—they must in this case al⟨so abandon⟩ their pretension of being friends to pea⟨ce. For⟩

such a conduct would be a violation ⟨of neutrality,⟩ which could not fail to produce war.

⟨It⟩ follows then that the ⟨proclamation⟩ is reconcilable with all that those ⟨who⟩ censure it contend for; taking them upon their own ground—that nothing is to be done incompatible with the preservation of Peace.

But though this would be a sufficient answer to the objection under consideration; yet it may not be without use to indulge some reflections on this very favourite topic of gratitude to France; since it is at this shrine we are continually invited to sacrifice the true interests of the Country; as if *"All for love and the world well lost"* were a fundamental maxim in politics.

Faith and Justice between nations are virtues of a nature sacred and un-equivocal. They cannot be too strongly inculcated nor too highly respected. Their obligations are definite and positive their utility unquestionable: they relate to objects, which with probity and sincerity generally admit of being brought within clear and intelligible rules.

But the same cannot be said of gratitude. It is not very often between nations, that it can be pronounced with certainty, that there exists a solid foundation for the sentiment—and how far it can justifiably be permitted to operate is always a question of still greater difficulty.

The basis of gratitude, is a benefit received or intended, which there was no right to claim, originating in a regard to the interest or advantage of the party, on whom the benefit is or is meant to be conferred. If a service is rendered from views *chiefly* relative to the immediate interest of the party, who renders it, and is productive of reciprocal advantages, there seems scarcely in such a case to be an adequate basis for a sentiment like that of gratitude. The effect would be disproportioned to the cause; if it ought to beget more than a disposition to render in turn a correspondent good office, founded on *mutual* interest and *reciprocal* advantage. But gratitude would require more than this; it would require, to a certain extent, even a sacrifice of the interest of the party obliged to the service or benefit of the party by whom the obligation had been conferred.

Between individuals, occasion is not unfrequently given to the exercise of gratitude. Instances of conferring benefits, from kind and benevolent dispositions or feelings towards the person benefitted, without any other interest on the part of the person, who confers the benefit, than the pleasure of doing a good action, occur every day among individuals. But among nations they perhaps never occur. It may be affirmed as a general principle, that the predominant motive of go⟨od⟩ offices from one nation to another is the interest or advantage of the Nation, which performs them.

Indeed the rule of morality is ⟨in⟩ this respect not exactly the same between Natio⟨ns⟩ as between individuals. The duty of making ⟨its⟩ own welfare the guide of its action⟨s⟩ is much stronger upon the former than upon the latter; in proportion to the greater magnitude and importance of national compared with individual happiness, to the greater permanency of the effects of national than of individual conduct. Existing Millions and for the most part future generations ar⟨e⟩ concerned in the present measures of a government: While the consequences of the private actions of ⟨an⟩ individual, for the most part, terminate with himself or are circumscribed within a narrow compass.

Whence it follows, that an individual may on numerous occasions meritoriously indulge the emotions of generosity and benevolence; not only without an eye to, but even at the expence of his own interest. But a Nation can rarely be justified in pursuing ⟨a similar⟩ course; and when it does so ought to confine itself within much stricter bounds.* Good offices, which are indifferent to the Interest of a Nation performing them, or which are compensated by the existence or expectation of some reasonable equivalent or which produce an essential good to the nation, to which they are rendered, without real detriment to the affairs of the nation rendering them, prescribe the limits of national generosity or benevolence.

It is not meant here to advocate a policy absolutely selfish or interested in nations; but to shew that a policy regulated by their own interest, as far as justice and good faith permit, is, and ought to be their prevailing policy:

---

*This conclusion derives confirmation from the reflection, that under every form of government, RULERS are only TRUSTEES for the happiness and interest of their nation, and cannot, consistently with their trust, follow the suggestions of kindness or humanity towards others, to the prejudice of their constituent.

and that either to ascribe to them a different principle of action, or to deduce from the supposition of it arguments for a self-denying and self-sacrificing gratitude on the part of a Nation, which may have received from another good offices, is to misconceive or mistake what usually are and ought to be the springs of National Conduct.

These general reflections will be auxiliary to a just estimate of our real situation with regard to France; of which a close view will be taken in a succeeding Paper.

Hamilton counters the argument that gratitude is due to France by analyzing the motives for assistance rendered in the American Revolution. Moreover, any gratitude is owed to Louis XVI rather than to the authors of the French Revolution.

Pacificus Number V

[Philadelphia, July 13–17, 1793]

France, the rival, time immemorial, of Great Britain, had in the course of the war, which ended in 1763, suffered from the successful arms of the latter the severest losses and the most mortifying defeats. Britain from that moment had acquired an ascendant over France in the affairs of Europe and in the commerce of the world, too decided to be endured without impatience, or without an eager desire of finding a favourable opportunity to destroy it and repair the breach which had been made in the National Glory. The animosity of wounded pride conspired with calculations of the interest of the State to give a keen edge to that impatience and to that desire.

The American Revolution offered the occasion. It attracted early the notice of France, though with extreme circumspection. As far as countenance and aid may be presumed to have been given prior to the epoch of the acknowlegement of our independence, it will be no unkind derogation to assert that they were marked neither with liberality nor with vigour; that they bore the appearance rather of a desire to keep alive disturbances, which would embarrass a rival Power, than of a serious design to assist a revolution or a serious expectation that it would be effected.

Reprinted with permission from *The Papers of Alexander Hamilton*, ed. Harold Syrett et al., vol. 15 (New York: Columbia University Press, 1969), 90–95.

The victories of Saratoga, the capture of an army, which went a great way towards deciding the issue of the contest, decided also the hesitations of France. They established in the government of that Country a confidence in our ability to accomplish our purpose; and as a consequence of it produced the treaties of alliance and commerce.

It is impossible ⟨to see⟩ in all this any thing more than the co⟨nd⟩uct of a rival nation; e⟨mb⟩racing a most promising opportunity to repress the pride and diminish the dangerous power of its rival by seconding a successful resistance to its authority, and by lopping off a valuable portion of its dominions. The dismemberment of this country from Great Britain was an obvious and a very important interest of France. It cannot be doubted, that it was the determining motive, and an adequate compensation for the assistance afforded us.

Men of sense, in this country, deduced an encouragement to the part, which their zeal for liberty prompted them to take in our Revolution, from the probability of the cooperation of France and Spain. It will be remembered that this argument was used in the publications of the day; but upon what was it bottomed? Upon the known competition between those Powers and ⟨Great⟩ Britain, upon their evident interest to reduce her power and circumscribe her empire; not upon motives of regard to our interest or of attac⟨hment⟩ to our cause. W⟨hoever⟩ should have alleged the latter, as grounds of the expectation held out, would have been justly considered as a Visionary, or a Deceiver. And whoever shall now ascribe the aid we received to such motives would not deserve to be viewed in a better light.

The inference from these facts is not obscure. Aid and co[o]peration founded upon a great interest, *pursued* and *obtained* by the party affording them, is not a proper stock upon which to en⟨graft⟩ that enthusiastic gratitude, which is claimed fr⟨om us⟩ by those *who love France more than the United States.*

This view of the subject, extorted by the extravagancy of such a claim, is not meant to disparage the just pretensions of France upon our *good will.* Though neither in the *motives* to the succours which she furnished us, nor in their *extent* (considering how powerfully *the point of honor in such a war* reinforced the considerations of interest, when she was once engaged) can be found a sufficient basis for that gratitude which is the theme of so much declamation. Yet we shall find in the manner of affording those succours just cause for our esteem and friendship.

France did not attempt, in the first instance, to take advantage of our situation to extort from us any humiliating or injurious concessions, as the price of her assistance; nor afterwards in the progress of the war, to impose hard terms as the condition of particular aids.

Though this course was certainly dictated by policy; yet it was an honorable and a magnanimous policy; such a one as always constitutes a title to the approbation and esteem of mankind and a claim to the friendship and acknowlegement of the party, in whose favour it is practiced.

But these sentiments are satisfied on the part of a Nation; when they produce sincere wishes for the happiness of the party, from whom it has experienced such conduct and a cordial disposition to *render all good and friendly offices which can be rendered without prejudice to its own solid and permanent interests.*

To ask of a Nation so situated, to make a sacrifice of substantial interest; to expose itself to the jealousy illwill or resentment of the rest of the world; to hazard in an eminent degree its own safety, for the benefit of the party, who may have observed towards it the conduct which has been discribed, would be to ask more than the nature of the case demands, more than the fundamental maxims of Society authorise, more than the dictates of sound reason justify.

A question has arisen, with regard to the proper object of that gratitude, which is so much insisted upon; whether the unfortunate Prince, by whom the assistance received was given; or the Nation of whom he was the Chief and the Organ.

The arguments which support the latter idea are as follow—

"Louis the XVI was but the constitutional Agent of the French Nation. He acted for and on behalf of the Nation; 'twas with their money and their blood he supported our cause. Tis to them therefore not to him, that our obligations are due. Louis the XVI in taking our part was no doubt actuated by motives of state-policy. An absolute Prince could not love liberty. But the people of France patronised our cause with zeal, from sympathy in its object. The people therefore, not the monarch, were intitled to our sympathy."

This reasoning may be ingenious but it is not founded in *nature* or *fact*.

Louis the XVI, though no more than the constitutional Agent of the Nation, had at the time the sole power of managing its affairs—the legal right of directing its will and its forces. It belonged to him to assist us or not, without consulting the nation; and he did assist us, without such consultation. His will alone was *active;* that of the Nation *passive.* If there was any kindness in the decision, demanding a return of kindness from us, it was the kindness of Louis the XVI—his heart was the depository of the sentiment. Let the genuine voice of nature then, unperverted by political subtleties, pronounce whether the acknowlegement, which may be due for that kindness, can be equitably transferred from him to others, who had no share in the decision—whether the *principle of gratitude* ought to determine us to behold with indifference his misfortunes and with satisfaction the triumphs of his enemies.

The doctrine that the Prince is only the Organ of his nation is conclusive to enforce the obligations of good faith between Nation and Nation; in other words, the observance of duties stipulated in treaties for National purposes—and it will even suffice to continue to a nation a claim to the friendship and good will of another resulting from friendly offices done by its prince; but it would be to carry it too far and to render it too artificial to attribute to it the effect of transferring that claim from the Prince to the Nation, by way of opposition and contrast. Friendship good will gratitude for favours received have so inseparable a reference to the motives with which and to the persons by whom they were rendered, as to be incapable of being transferred to *another* at *his expence.*

But Louis the XVI it is said, acted from reasons of State without regard to our cause; while the people of France patronised it with zeal and attachment.

As far as the assertion, with regard to the Monarch is founded and is an objection to our gratitude to him it destroys the whole fabric of gratitude to France; For our gratitude is and must be relative to the *services* rendered us. The Nation can only claim it on the score of their having been rendered *by their Agent with their means.* If the views with which he rendered them divested them of that merit which ought to inspire gratitude — none is due. The Nation no more than their Agent can claim it.

As to the individual good wishes of the citizens of France, as they did not produce the services rendered to us as a nation, they can be no foundation for national gratitude. They can only call for a reciprocation of individual good wishes. They cannot form the basis of public obligation.

But the assertion takes more for granted, than there is reason to believe true.

Louis the XVI no doubt took part in our contest from reasons of State; but Louis the 16 was a humane kind-hearted man. The acts of his youth had intitled him to this character. It is natural for a man of such a disposition to become interested in the cause of those whom he protects or aids; and if the concurrent testi⟨mony⟩ of the period may be creditted, there was no man in France more personally friendly to the cause of this Country than Louis the 16th. I am much misinformed, if repeated declarations of the venerable Franklin did not attest this fact.

It is a just tribute to the People of France to admit, that they manifested a lively interest in the cause of America; but while motives are scanned, who can say how much of it is to be ascribed to the antipathy which they bore to their rival neighbours — how much to their sympathy in the object of our pursuit? It is certain, that the love of liberty was not a *national* sentiment in France when a zeal for our cause first appeared among that people.

There is reason to believe too that the attachment to our cause, which ultimately became very extensive, if not general, did not originate with the mass of the French people. It began with the higher circles, more immediately connected with the government, and was thence transmitted through the Nation.

This observation, besides its tendency to correct ideas, which are calculated to give a false direction to the public feeling, may serve to check the spirit of illiberal invective, which has been wantonly indulged against those distinguished friends of America, who, though the Authors of the French Revolution, have fallen victims to it, because their principles would not permit them to go the length of an intire subversion of the monarchy.

The preachers of gratitude are not ashamed to brand *Louis* the XVI as a Tyrant, and *La Fayette* as a Traitor. But how can we wonder at this, when they insinuate a distrust even of a   !¹

In urging the friendly disposition of our cause manifested by the people of France, as a motive to our gratitude towards that people, it ought not to be forgotten, that those dispositions were not confined to the inhabitants of that Country. They were eminently shared by the people of the United Provinces, produced to us valuable pecuniary aids from their citizens and finally involved them in the war on the same side with us. It may be added, too, that here the patronage of our cause emphatically began with the community, not originating as in France, with the Government, but finally implicating the government in the consequences.

Our cause had also numerous friends in other countries; even in that with which we were at war. Conducted with prudence, moderation, justice and humanity, it may truly be said to have been a popular cause among mankind; conciliating the countenance of Princes and the affection of Nations.

The dispositions of the individual Citizens of France can therefore in no sense be urged, as constituting a peculiar claim to our gratitude. As far as there is foundation for it, it must be referred to the *services rendered;* and, in the first instance, ⟨to⟩ the unfortunate monarch, that rendered them. This is the conclusion ⟨of⟩ Nature and Reason.

[1. This space was left blank by Hamilton.]

Continuing the argument of the previous paper, the question discussed is the extent to which gratitude for aid in the American Revolution requires an American commitment in France's war with England. Hamilton continues to argue that gratitude in and of itself is not a sound principle for guiding foreign attachments; rather, the United States must strive for what is in the best interests of the nation, which is essentially a practical consideration. French aid in the American Revolution does not justify the sacrifice of substantial interests or the safety of the United States.

Pacificus Number VI

[Philadelphia, July 17, 1793]

The very men who not long since, with a holy zeal, would have been glad to make an *autos de fé* of any one who should have presumed to assign bounds to our obligations to Louis the XVI are now ready to consign to the flames those who venture even to think, that he died a proper object of our sympathy or regret. The greatest pains are taken to excite against him our detestation. His supposed perjuries and crimes are sounded in the public ear, with all the exaggerations of intemperate declaiming. All the *unproved* and *contradicted allegations* which have been brought against him are taken for granted, as the oracles of truth, on no better grounds, than the mere general presumptions—that he could not have been a friend to a revolution which stripped him of so much power—that it is not likely the Convention would have pronounced him guilty, and consigned him to so ignominious a fate, if he had been really innocent.

Reprinted with permission from *The Papers of Alexander Hamilton*, ed. Harold Syrett et al., vol. 15 (New York: Columbia University Press, 1969), 100–106.

It is very possible that time may disclose facts and proofs, which will substantiate the guilt imputed to Louis; but these facts and proofs have not yet been authenticated to the world; and justice admonishes us to wait for their production and authentication.

Those who have most closely attended to the course of the transaction, find least cause to be convinced of the criminality of the deceased monarch. While his counsel, whose characters give weight to their assertions, with an air of conscious truth, boldly appeal to facts and proofs, in the knowledge and possession of the Convention, for the refutation of the charges brought against him—the members of that body, in all the debates upon the subject which have reached this country, either directly from France, or circuitously through England, appear to have contented themselves with *assuming* the existence of the facts charged, and inferring from them a criminality which, after the abolition of the royalty, they were interested to establish.

The presumptions of guilt drawn from the suggestions which have been stated, are more than counterbalanced by an opposite presumption, which is too obvious not to have occurred to many, though I do not recollect yet to have met with it in print. It is this:

If the Convention had possessed *clear evidence* of the guilt of Louis, they wou'd have promulgated it to the world in an *authentic* and *unquestionable* shape. Respect for the opinion of mankind, regard for their own character, the interest of their cause made this an *indispensable* duty; nor can the omission be satisfactorily ascribed to any other reason, than the want of *such evidence*.

The inference from this is, that the melancholy catastrophe of Louis XVI, was the result of a supposed political expediency, rather than of real criminality.

In a case so circumstanced, does it, can it consist with our justice or our humanity, to partake in the angry and vindictive passions which are endeavored to be excited against the unfortunate monarch? Was it a crime in him to have been born a Prince? Could this circumstance forfeit his title to the commiseration due to his misfortunes as a man?

Would *gratitude* dictate to a people, situated as are the people of this country, to *lend their aid* to extend to the son the misfortunes of the father? Should we not be more certain of violating no obligation of that kind—of not implicating the delicacy of our national character—by taking no part in the contest—than by throwing our weight into either scale?

Would not a just estimate of the origin and progress of our relations to France, viewed with reference to the mere question of gratitude, lead us to this result—that we ought not to *take part* against the son and successor of a father, on whose *sole will* depended the assistance which we received— that we ought not to *take part* with him against the nation, whose blood and whose treasure had been, in the hands of the father, the means of the assistance afforded us?

But we are sometimes told, by way of answer, that the cause of France is the cause of liberty: and that we are bound to assist the nation on the score of their being engaged in the defence of that cause. How far this idea ought to carry us, will be the object of future examination.

It is only necessary here to observe, that it presents a question essentially different from that which has been in discussion. If we are bound to assist the French nation, on the principle of their being embarked in the defence of liberty, this is a ground altogether foreign to that of gratitude. Gratitude has reference only *to kind offices received.* The obligation to assist the cause of liberty, has reference to the merits of that cause, and to the interest we have in its support. It is possible, that the benefactor may be on one side—the defenders and supporters of liberty on the other. Gratitude may point one way—the love of liberty another. It is therefore important to just conclusions, not to confound the two things.

A sentiment of justice more than the importance of the question itself has led to so particular a discussion, respecting the proper object of whatever acknowledgment may be due from the United States for the aid which they received from France during their own revolution.

The extent of the obligation which it may impose is by far the most interesting enquiry. And though it is presumed, that enough has been already said to evince, that it does in no degree require us to embark in the war; yet there is another and very simple view of the subject, which is too convincing to be omitted.

The assistance lent us by France was afforded by a great and powerful nation, possessing numerous armies, a respectable fleet, and the means of rendering it a match for the force to be contended with. The position of Europe was favorable to the enterprise; a general disposition prevailing to see the power of Great-Britain abridged. The co-operation of Spain was very much a matter of course, and the probability of other powers becoming engaged on the same side not remote. Great Britain was alone and likely to continue so—France had a great and persuasive interest in the separation of this country from Britain. In this situation with *much to hope* and *not much to fear,* she took part in our quarrel.

France is at this time *singly* engaged with the greatest part of Europe, in-cluding all the first rate powers, except one, and in danger of being engaged with all the rest. To use the emphatic language of a member of the National Convention—she has but *one enemy* and that is ALL EUROPE. Her internal affairs are *without doubt* in serious disorder. Her navy comparatively incon-siderable. The United States are a young nation; their population though rapidly increasing, still small—their resources, though growing, not great; without armies, without fleets—capable from the nature of the country and the spirit of its inhabitants of immense exertions for self-defence, but little capable of those external efforts which could materially serve the cause of France. So far from having any direct interest in going to war, they have the strongest motives of interest to avoid it. By embarking with France in the war, they would have incomparably more to apprehend, than to hope.

This contrast of situations and inducements is alone a conclusive demon-stration, that the United States are not under an obligation, from gratitude, to join France in the war. The utter disparity between the circumstances of the service *to be rendered,* and of the *service received,* proves, that the one cannot be an adequate basis of obligation for the other. There would be a want of equality, and consequently of reciprocity.

But complete justice would not be done to this question of gratitude, were no notice to be taken of the address, which has appeared in the public papers (the authenticity of which has not been impeached) from the Convention of France to the United States; announcing the appointment of the present Minister Plenipotentiary. In that address the Convention informs us, that "the support which the ancient French Court had afforded the United States to recover their independence, was only the fruit of a base speculation; and that their glory offended its ambitious views, and the Ambassadors of France bore the criminal orders of stopping the career of their prosperity."

[If this information is to be admitted in the full force of the terms, it is very fatal to the claim of gratitude towards France. An observation similar to one made in a former paper occurs here. If the organ of the Nation, on whose will the aid given us depended, acted not only from motives irrelative to our advantage but from unworthy motives or as it is stated, from a *base* speculation; if afterwards he displayed a temper hostile to the confirmation of our security and prosperity, in a point so momentous as the establishment of a more adequate government; he acquired no title to our gratitude in the first instance, or he forfeited it in the second. And the Nation of France, who can only claim it in virtue of the conduct of their agent must together with him renounce the pretension. It is an obvious principle, that if a Nation can claim merit from the good deeds of its sovereign, it must answer for the demerit of his misdeeds. The rule to be a good one, must apply both ways.

But some deductions are to be made from the suggestions contained in the address of the Convention in reference to the motives which evidently dictated the communication. Their zeal to alienate the good will of this country from the late monarch and to increase the odium of the French Nation against the monarchy which was so ardent as to make them overlook the tendency of their communication to disarm their votaries among us of the plea of gratitude, may justly be suspected of exaggeration.

The truth probably is, that the *base speculation* charged amounts to nothing more than the Government of France in affording us assistance was directed by the motives which have been attributed to it, namely, the desire of promoting the interest of France, by lessening the power of Great

Britain and opening a new channel of commerce to herself—that the] orders said to have been given to the Ambassadors of France to stop the career of our prosperity are [resolvable into a speculative jealousy of the Ministers of the day, lest the UStates by becoming as powerful and great as they are capable of becoming under an efficient government might prove formidable to the European possessions in America. With these qualifications and allowances the address offers no new discovery to the intelligent and unbiased friends of their Country. They knew long ago, that the interest of France had been the governing motive of the aid afforded us; and they saw clearly enough, in the conversation & conduct of her Agents, while the present constitution of the United States was under consideration, that the Government, of which they were the instruments, would have preferred our remaining under the old form, for the reason which has been stated.] They perceived also, [that these views had their effect upon some of the devoted partisans of France among ourselves; as they now perceive that the same characters are embodying themselves with all the aid they can obtain, under the like influence, to resist the *operation* of that government of which they withstood the establishment.]

All this was and is seen, and the body of the people of America are too discerning to be long in the dark about it. Too wise to have been misled by foreign or domestic machinations, they adopted a constitution which was necessary to their safety and to their happiness. Too wise still to be ensnared by the same machinations, they will support the government they have established, and will take care of their own peace, in spite of the insidious efforts which are making to detach them from the one, and to disturb the other.

The information which the address of the Convention contains, ought to serve as an instructive lesson to the people of this country. It ought to teach us not to over-rate *foreign friendships*—to be upon our guard against *foreign attachments*. The former will generally be found hollow and delusive; the latter will have a natural tendency to lead us aside from our own true interest, and to make us the dupes of foreign influence. They introduce a principle of action, which in its effects, if the expression may be allowed, is *anti-national.* Foreign influence is truly the GRECIAN HORSE to a re-public. We cannot be too careful to exclude its entrance. Nor ought we to imagine, that it can only make its approaches in the gross form of direct bribery. It is then most dangerous, when it comes under the patronage of our passions, under the auspices of national prejudice and partiality.

I trust the morals of this country are yet too good to leave much to ap-prehend on the score of bribery. Caresses, condescentions, flattery, in uni-son with our prepossessions, are infinitely more to be feared; and as far as there is opportunity for corruption, it is to be remembered, that one foreign power can employ this resource as well as another, and that the effect must be much greater, when it is combined with the other means of influence, than where it stands alone.

PACIFICUS

Hamilton answers Madison's objections regarding the prudence of a neutrality proclamation. His answer constitutes a summary statement of the American position.

Pacificus Number VII

[Philadelphia, July 27, 1793]

The remaining objection to the Proclamation of Neutrality, still to be discussed, is that it was [out of time and unnecessary.]

To give colour to this *objection* it is asked—why did not the Proclamation appear when the war commenced with Austria & Prussia? Why was it forborne till Great Britain Holland and Spain became engaged? Why did not the Government wait till the arrival at Philadelphia of the Minister of the French Republic? Why did it volunteer a declaration not required of it by any of the belligerent Parties?

To most of these questions solid answers have already appeared in the public Prints. Little more can be done than to repeat and enforce them.

Austria and Prussia are not Maritime Powers. Contraventions of neutrality as against them were not likely to take place to any extent or in a shape that would attract their notice. It would therefore have been useless, if not ridiculous, to have made formal Declaration on the subject, while they were the only parties opposed to France.

But the reverse of this is the case with regard to Spain Holland & England. These are all commercial maritime Nations. It was to be expected, that their attention would be immediately drawn towards the UStates with sensibility, and even with jealousy. It was to be feared that some of our citizens

Reprinted with permission from *The Papers of Alexander Hamilton,* ed. Harold Syrett et al., vol. 15 (New York: Columbia University Press, 1969), 130–35.

might be tempted by the prospect of gain to go into measures which would injure them, and commit the peace of the Country. Attacks by some of these Powers upon the possessions of France in America were to be looked for as a matter of course. While the views of the UStates as to that particular, were problematical, they would naturally consider us as a power that might become their enemy. This they would have been the more apt to do, on account of those public demonstrations of attachment to the cause of France; of which there has been so great a display. Jealousy, every body knows, especially if sharpened by resentment; is apt to lead to ill treatment, ill treatment to hostility.

In proportion to the probability of our being regarded with a suspicious and consequently an unfriendly eye, by the Powers at war with France; in proportion to the danger of imprudencies being committed by any of our citizens, which might occasion a rupture with them—the policy on the part of the Government of removing all doubt as to its own disposition, and of deciding the condition of the UStates in the view of the parties concerned became obvious and urgent.

Were the UStates now what, if we do not rashly throw away the advantages we possess, they may expect to be in 15 or 20 years, there would have been more room for an insinuation which has been thrown out namely that they ought to have secured to themselves some advantage, as the consideration of their neutrality; an idea however of which the justice and magnanimity cannot be commended. But in their present situation, with their present strength and resources, an attempt of that kind could have only served to display pretensions at once excessive and unprincipled. The chance of obtaining any collateral advantage, if such a chance there was, by leaving a doubt upon our intentions as to peace or war could not wisely have been put for a single instant in competition with the tendency of a contrary conduct to secure our peace.

The conduciveness of the Declaration of neutrality to that end was not the only recommendation to an early adoption of the measure. It was of great importance that our own citizens should understand, as soon as possible, the opinion which the Government entertained of the nature of our relations to the warring parties and of the propriety or expediency of our taking a side or remaining neuter. The arrangements of our merchants could not but be very differently affected by the one hypothesis, or the other; and it would necessarily have been very detrimental and perplexing to them to have been left in uncertainty. It is not requisite to say how much our agriculture and other interests would have been likely to have suffered by embarrassments to our Merchants.

The idea of its having been incumbent on the Government to delay the measure, for the coming of the Minister of the French Republic, is as absurd as it is humiliating. Did the Executive stand in need of the logic of a foreign Agent to enlighten it either as to the duties or the interests of the Nation? Or was it bound to ask his consent to a step which appeared to itself consistent with the former and conducive to the latter?

The sense of our treaties was to be learnt from the treaties themselves. It was not difficult to pronounce beforehand that we had a greater interest in the preservation of Peace, than in any advantages with which France might tempt our participation in the war. Commercial privileges were all that she could offer, of real value in our estimation, and a *carte blanche* on this head would have been an inadequate recompence for renouncing peace and committing ourselves voluntarily to the chances of so precarious and perilous a war. Besides, if the privileges which might have been conceded were not founded in a real permanent mutual interest—of what value would be the Treaty, that should concede them? Ought not the calculation in such case, to be upon a speedy resumption of them, with perhaps a quarrel as the pretext? On the other hand may we not trust that commercial privileges, which are truly founded in mutual interest will grow out of that interest; without the necessity of giving a premium for them at the expence of our peace?

To what purpose then was the Executive to have waited for the arrival of the Minister? Was it to give opportunity to contentious discussions—to intriguing machinations—to the clamors of a faction won to a foreign interest?

Whether the Declaration of Neutrality issued upon or without the requisition of any of the belligerent Powers can only be known to their respective Ministers and to the proper Officers of our Government. But if it be true that it issued without any such requisition, it is an additional indication of the wisdom of the measure.

It is of much importance to the end of preserving peace, that the Belligerent Powers should be thoroughly convinced of the sincerity of our intentions to observe the neutrality we profess; and it cannot fail to have weight in producing this conviction that the Declaration of it was a spontaneous Act—not stimulated by any requisition on the part of either of them—proceeding purely from our own view of our duty and interest.

It was not surely necessary for the Government to wait for such a requisition; while there were advantages and no disadvantages in anticipating it. The benefit of an early notification to our merchants, conspired with the consideration just mentioned to recommend the course which was pursued.

If, in addition to the rest, the early manifestation of the views of the Government has had any effect in fixing the public opinion on the subject and in counteracting the success of the efforts which it was to be foreseen would be made to disunite it, this alone would be a great recommendation of the policy of having suffered no delay to intervene.

What has been already said in this and in preceding papers affords a full answer to the suggestion that the proclamation was unnecessary. It would be a waste of time to add any thing more.

But there has been a criticism, several times repeated, which may deserve a moment's attention. It has been urged, that the Proclamation ought to have contained some reference to our Treaties, and that the generality of the promise to observe a conduct *friendly* and *impartial* towards the belligerent powers ought to have been qualified with the expressions equivalent to these—"*as far as may consist with the Treaties of the Ustates.*"

The insertion of such a clause would have entirely defeated the object of the Proclamation, by rendering the intention of the Government equivocal. That object was to assure the Powers at War and our own Citizens, that in the opinion of the Executive it was consistent with the duty and interest of the Nation to observe a neutrality in the War and that it was intended to pursue a conduct corresponding with that opinion. Words equivalent to those contended for would have rendered the other part of the Declaration nugatory; by *leaving it uncertain whether the Executive did or did not believe a state of Neutrality to be consistent with our Treaties.* Neither foreign Powers nor our own citizens would have been able to have drawn any conclusion from the Proclamation; and both would have had a right to consider it as a mere equivocation.

By not inserting any such ambiguous expressions, the Proclamation was susceptible of an intelligible and proper construction. While it denoted on the one hand, that in the judgment of the Executive, there was nothing in our treaties obliging us *to become a party in the war,* it left it to be expected on the other—that all stipulations compatible with neutrality, according to the laws and usages of Nations, would be enforced. It follows, that the Proclamation was in this particular exactly what it ought to have been.

The words "make known the disposition of the UStates" have also given a handle to cavil. It has been asked how could the President undertake to declare the disposition of the UStates. The People for aught he knew may have been in a very different sentiment. Thus a conformity with republican propriety and modesty is turned into a topic of accusation.

Had the President announced his own disposition, he would have been chargeable with egotism if not presumption. The constitutional organ of intercourse between the UStates & foreign Nations—whenever he speaks to them, it is in that capacity; it is in the name and on behalf of the UStates. It must therefore be with greater propriety that he speaks of their disposition than of his own.

It is easy to imagine, that occasions frequently occur in the communications to foreign Governments and foreign Agents—which render it necessary to speak of the friendship or *friendly disposition* of the U States, of *their disposition* to cultivate harmony and good understanding, to reciprocate neighbourly offices &c. &c. It is usual for example when public Ministers are received, for some complimentary expressions to be interchanged. It is presumeable that the late reception of the French Minister did not pass, without some assurance on the part of the President of the friendly disposition of the UStates towards France. Admitting it to have happened, would it be deemed an improper arrogation? If not, why it was more so, to declare the disposition of the UStates to observe a neutrality in the existing War?

In all such cases nothing more is to be understood than an official expression of the *political* disposition of the Nation *inferred* from its political relations obligations and interests. It is never to be supposed that the expression is meant to convey the precise state of the Individual sentiments or opinions of the great mass of the People.

Kings and Princes speak of their own dispositions. The Majistrates of Republics of the dispositions of their Nations. The President therefore has evidently used the style adapted to his situation & the Criticism upon it is plainly a cavil.

PACIFICUS

Thomas Jefferson to James Madison

DEAR SIR   JULY 7. 1793

I wrote you on the 30th. ult. and shall be uneasy till I have heard you have received it. I have no letter from you this week. You will perceive by the inclosed papers that they are to be discontinued in their present form & a daily paper published in their stead, *if subscribers enough can be obtained.* I fear they cannot, for nobody here scarcely has ever taken his paper. You will see in these Colo. H's 2d. & 3d. pacificus. Nobody answers him, & his doctrine will therefore be taken for confessed. For god's sake, my dear Sir, take up your pen, select the most striking heresies, and cut him to peices in the face of the public. There is nobody else who can & will enter the lists with him. Never in my opinion, was so calamitous an appointment made, as that of the present minister of F. here. Hotheaded, all imagination, no judgment, passionate, disrespectful & even indecent towards the P. in his written as well as verbal communications, talking of appeals from him to Congress, from them to the people, urging the most unreasonable & groundless propositions, & in the most dictatorial style &c. &c. &c. If ever it should be necessary to lay his communications before Congress or the public, they will excite universal indignation. He renders my position immensely difficult. He does me justice personally, and, giving him time to vent himself & then cool, I am on a footing to advise him freely, & he respects it. But he breaks out again on the very first occasion, so as to shew that he is incapable of correcting himself. To complete our misfortune we have no channel of our own through which we can correct the irritating representations he may make. Adieu. Yours affectionately.

Reprinted with permission from *The Papers of James Madison,* ed. Thomas A. Mason, Robert A. Rutland, and Jeanne K. Sisson, vol. 15 (Charlottesville: University Press of Virginia, 1985), 43.

Madison's focus is on a strict construction of executive power. He argues here that the power to declare war and make treaties can never fall within the definition of executive powers. The natural province of the executive is to execute laws, as that of the legislature is to make laws. Therefore all executive acts must presuppose the existence of laws to be executed. To say that the making of treaties, being substantially of a legislative nature, belongs to the executive is to say that the executive possesses a legislative power. The power to declare war is subject to the same reasoning.

Helvidius Number I

[24 August 1793]

Several pieces with the signature of PACIFICUS were lately published, which have been read with singular pleasure and applause, by the foreigners and degenerate citizens among us, who hate our republican government, and the French revolution; whilst the publication seems to have been too little regarded, or too much despised by the steady friends to both.

Had the doctrines inculcated by the writer, with the natural consequences from them, been nakedly presented to the public, this treatment might have been proper. Their true character would then have struck every eye, and been rejected by the feelings of every heart. But they offer themselves to the reader in the dress of an elaborate dissertation; they are mingled with a few truths that may serve them as a passport to credulity; and they are introduced with professions of anxiety for the preservation of peace, for the

Reprinted with permission from *The Papers of James Madison,* ed. Thomas A. Mason, Robert A. Rutland, and Jeanne K. Sisson, vol. 15 (Charlottesville: University Press of Virginia, 1985), 66–73.

welfare of the government, and for the respect due to the present head of the executive, that may prove a snare to patriotism.

In these disguises they have appeared to claim the attention I propose to bestow on them; with a view to shew, from the publication itself, that under colour of vindicating an important public act, of a chief magistrate, who enjoys the confidence and love of his country, principles are advanced which strike at the vitals of its constitution, as well as at its honor and true interest.

As it is not improbable that attempts may be made to apply insinuations which are seldom spared when particular purposes are to be answered, to the author of the ensuing observations, it may not be improper to premise, that he is a friend to the constitution, that he wishes for the preservation of peace, and that the present chief magistrate has not a fellow-citizen, who is penetrated with deeper respect for his merits, or feels a purer solicitude for his glory.

This declaration is made with no view of courting a more favorable ear to what may be said than it deserves. The sole purpose of it is, to obviate imputations which might weaken the impressions of truth; and which are the more likely to be resorted to, in proportion as solid and fair arguments may be wanting.

The substance of the first piece, sifted from its inconsistencies and its vague expressions, may be thrown into the following propositions:

That the powers of declaring war and making treaties are, in their nature, executive powers:

That being particularly vested by the constitution in other departments, they are to be considered as exceptions out of the general grant to the executive department:

That being, as exceptions, to be construed strictly, the powers not strictly within them, remain with the executive:

That the executive consequently, as the organ of intercourse with foreign nations, and the interpreter and executor of treaties, and the law of nations, is authorised, to expound all articles of treaties, those involving questions of war and peace, as well as others; to judge of the obligations of the United

States to make war or not, under any casus federis or eventual operation of the contract, relating to war; and, to pronounce the state of things resulting from the obligations of the United States, as understood by the executive:

That in particular the executive had authority to judge whether in the case of the mutual guaranty between the United States and France, the former were bound by it to engage in the war:

That the executive has, in pursuance of that authority, decided that the United States are not bound: And,

That its proclamation of the 22d of April last, is to be taken as the effect and expression of that decision.

The basis of the reasoning is, we perceive, the extraordinary doctrine, that the powers of making war and treaties, are in their nature executive; and therefore comprehended in the general grant of executive power, where not specially and strictly excepted out of the grant.

Let us examine this doctrine; and that we may avoid the possibility of mistating the writer, it shall be laid down in his own words: a precaution the more necessary, as scarce any thing else could outweigh the improbability, that so extravagant a tenet should be hazarded, at so early a day, in the face of the public.

His words are—"Two of these (exceptions and qualifications to the executive powers) have been already noticed—the participation of the Senate in the *appointment of officers,* and the *making of treaties.* A *third* remains to be mentioned—the right of the legislature to *declare war, and grant letters of marque and reprisal.*"

Again—"It deserves to be remarked, that as the participation of the Senate in the *making treaties,* and the power of the legislature to *declare war,* are *exceptions* out of the general *executive power,* vested in the President, they are to be construed *strictly,* and ought to be extended no farther than is essential to their execution."

If there be any countenance to these positions, it must be found either 1st, in the writers, of authority, on public law; or 2d, in the quality and operation of the powers to make war and treaties; or 3d, in the constitution of the United States.

It would be of little use to enter far into the first source of information, not only because our own reason and our own constitution, are the best guides; but because a just analysis and discrimination of the powers of government, according to their executive, legislative and judiciary qualities are not to be expected in the works of the most received jurists, who wrote before a critical attention was paid to those objects, and with their eyes too much on monarchical governments, where all powers are confounded in the sovereignty of the prince. It will be found however, I believe, that all of them, particularly Wolfius, Burlamaqui and Vattel, speak of the powers to declare war, to conclude peace, and to form alliances, as among the highest acts of the sovereignty; of which the legislative power must at least be an integral and preeminent part.

Writers, such as Locke and Montesquieu, who have discussed more particularly the principles of liberty and the structure of government, lie under the same disadvantage, of having written before these subjects were illuminated by the events and discussions which distinguish a very recent period. Both of them too are evidently warped by a regard to the particular government of England, to which one of them owed allegiance;* and the other professed an admiration bordering on idolatry. Montesquieu, however, has rather distinguished himself by enforcing the reasons and the importance of avoiding a confusion of the several powers of government, than by enumerating and defining the powers which belong to each particular class. And Locke, notwithstanding the early date of his work on civil government, and the example of his own government before his eyes, admits that the particular powers in question, which, after some of the writers on public law he calls *federative*, are really *distinct* from the *executive*, though almost always united with it, and *hardly to be separated into distinct hands.* Had he not lived under a monarchy, in which these powers were united; or had he written by the lamp which truth now presents to lawgivers, the last observation would probably never have dropt from his pen. But let us quit

* *The chapter on prerogative, shews how much the reason of the philosopher was clouded by the royalism of the Englishman.*

a field of research which is more likely to perplex than to decide, and bring the question to other tests of which it will be more easy to judge.

2. If we consult for a moment, the nature and operation of the two powers to declare war and make treaties, it will be impossible not to see that they can never fall within a proper definition of executive powers. The natural province of the executive magistrate is to execute laws, as that of the legislature is to make laws. All his acts therefore, properly executive, must pre-suppose the existence of the laws to be executed. A treaty is not an execution of laws: it does not pre-suppose the existence of laws. It is, on the contrary, to have itself the force of a *law,* and to be carried into *execution,* like all *other laws,* by the *executive magistrate.* To say then that the power of making treaties which are confessedly laws, belongs naturally to the department which is to execute laws, is to say, that the executive department naturally includes a legislative power. In theory, this is an absurdity—in practice a tyranny.

The power to declare war is subject to similar reasoning. A declaration that there shall be war, is not an execution of laws: it does not suppose pre-existing laws to be executed: it is not in any respect, an act merely executive. It is, on the contrary, one of the most deliberative acts that can be performed; and when performed, has the effect of *repealing* all the *laws* operating in a state of peace, so far as they are inconsistent with a state of war: and of *enacting* as *a rule for the executive,* a *new code* adapted to the relation between the society and its foreign enemy. In like manner a conclusion of peace *annuls* all the *laws* peculiar to a state of war, and *revives* the general *laws* incident to a state of peace.

These remarks will be strengthened by adding that treaties, particularly treaties of peace, have sometimes the effect of changing not only the external laws of the society, but operate also on the internal code, which is purely municipal, and to which the legislative authority of the country is of itself competent and compleat.

From this view of the subject it must be evident, that although the executive may be a convenient organ of preliminary communications with foreign governments, on the subjects of treaty or war; and the proper agent for carrying into execution the final determinations of the competent authority;

yet it can have no pretensions from the nature of the powers in question compared with the nature of the executive trust, to that essential agency which gives validity to such determinations.

It must be further evident that, if these powers be not in their nature purely legislative, they partake so much more of that, than of any other quality, that under a constitution leaving them to result to their most natural department, the legislature would be without a rival in its claim.

Another important inference to be noted is, that the powers of making war and treaty being substantially of a legislative, not an executive nature, the rule of interpreting exceptions strictly, must narrow instead of enlarging executive pretensions on those subjects.

3.   It remains to be enquired whether there be any thing in the constitution itself which shews that the powers of making war and peace are considered as of an executive nature, and as comprehended within a general grant of executive power.

It will not be pretended that this appears from any *direct* position to be found in the instrument.

If it were *deducible* from any particular expressions it may be presumed that the publication would have saved us the trouble of the research.

Does the doctrine then result from the actual distribution of powers among the several branches of the government? Or from any fair analogy between the powers of war and treaty and the enumerated powers vested in the executive alone?

Let us examine.

In the general distribution of powers, we find that of declaring war expressly vested in the Congress, where every other legislative power is declared to be vested, and without any other qualification than what is common to every other legislative act. The constitutional idea of this power would seem then clearly to be, that it is of a legislative and not an executive nature.

This conclusion becomes irresistible, when it is recollected, that the constitution cannot be supposed to have placed either any power legislative in its nature, entirely among executive powers, or any power executive in its nature, entirely among legislative powers, without charging the constitution, with that kind of intermixture and consolidation of different powers, which would violate a fundamental principle in the organization of free governments. If it were not unnecessary to enlarge on this topic here, it could be shewn, that the constitution was originally vindicated, and has been constantly expounded, with a disavowal of any such intermixture.

The power of treaties is vested jointly in the President and in the Senate, which is a branch of the legislature. From this arrangement merely, there can be no inference that would necessarily exclude the power from the executive class: since the senate is joined with the President in another power, that of appointing to offices, which as far as relate to executive offices at least, is considered as of an executive nature. Yet on the other hand, there are sufficient indications that the power of treaties is regarded by the constitution as materially different from mere executive power, and as having more affinity to the legislative than to the executive character.

One circumstance indicating this, is the constitutional regulation under which the senate give their consent in the case of treaties. In all other cases the consent of the body is expressed by a majority of voices. In this particular case, a concurrence of two thirds at least is made necessary, as a substitute or compensation for the other branch of the legislature, which on certain occasions, could not be conveniently a party to the transaction.

But the conclusive circumstance is, that treaties when formed according to the constitutional mode, are confessedly to have the force and operation of *laws,* and are to be a rule for the courts in controversies between man and man, as much as any *other laws.* They are even emphatically declared by the constitution to be "the supreme law of the land."

So far the argument from the constitution is precisely in opposition to the doctrine. As little will be gained in its favour from a comparison of the two powers, with those particularly vested in the President alone.

As there are but few it will be most satisfactory to review them one by one.

"The President shall be commander in chief of the army and navy of the United States, and of the militia when called into the actual service of the United States."

There can be no relation worth examining between this power and the general power of making treaties. And instead of being analogous to the power of declaring war, it affords a striking illustration of the incompatibility of the two powers in the same hands. Those who are to *conduct a war* cannot in the nature of things, be proper or safe judges, whether *a war ought* to be *commenced, continued,* or *concluded.* They are barred from the latter functions by a great principle in free government, analogous to that which separates the sword from the purse, or the power of executing from the power of enacting laws.

"He may require the opinion in writing of the principal officers in each of the executive departments upon any subject relating to the duties of their respective offices; and he shall have power to grant reprieves and pardons for offences against the United States, except in case of impeachment." These powers can have nothing to do with the subject.

"The President shall have power to fill up vacancies that may happen during the recess of the senate, by granting commissions which shall expire at the end of the next session." The same remark is applicable to this power, as also to that of "receiving ambassadors, other public ministers and consuls." The particular use attempted to be made of this last power will be considered in another place.

"He shall take care that the laws shall be faithfully executed and shall commission all officers of the United States." To see the laws faithfully executed constitutes the essence of the executive authority. But what relation has it to the power of making treaties and war, that is, of determining what the *laws shall be* with regard to other nations? No other certainly than what subsists between the powers of executing and enacting laws; no other consequently, than what forbids a coalition of the powers in the same department.

I pass over the few other specified functions assigned to the President, such as that of convening of the legislature, &c. &c. which cannot be drawn into the present question.

It may be proper however to take notice of the power of removal from office, which appears to have been adjudged to the President by the laws establishing the executive departments; and which the writer has endeavoured to press into his service. To justify any favourable inference from this case, it must be shewn, that the powers of war and treaties are of a kindred nature to the power of removal, or at least are equally within a grant of executive power. Nothing of this sort has been attempted, nor probably will be attempted. Nothing can in truth be clearer, than that no analogy, or shade of analogy, can be traced between a power in the supreme officer responsible for the faithful execution of the laws, to displace a subaltern officer employed in the execution of the laws; and a power to make treaties, and to declare war, such as these have been found to be in their nature, their operation, and their consequences.

Thus it appears that by whatever standard we try this doctrine, it must be condemned as no less vicious in theory than it would be dangerous in practice. It is countenanced neither by the writers on law; nor by the nature of the powers themselves; nor by any general arrangements or particular expressions, or plausible analogies, to be found in the constitution.

Whence then can the writer have borrowed it?

There is but one answer to this question.

The power of making treaties and the power of declaring war, are *royal prerogatives* in the *British government,* and are accordingly treated as Executive prerogatives by *British commentators.*

We shall be the more confirmed in the necessity of this solution of the problem, by looking back to the aera of the constitution, and satisfying ourselves that the writer could not have been misled by the doctrines maintained by our own commentators on our own government. That I may not ramble beyond prescribed limits, I shall content myself with an extract from a work which entered into a systematic explanation and defence of the constitution, and to which there has frequently been ascribed some influence in conciliating the public assent to the government in the form proposed. Three circumstances conspire in giving weight to this cotemporary exposition. It was made at a time when no application to *persons* or *measures* could bias: The opinion given was not transiently mentioned, but formally and critically elucidated: It related to a point in the constitution which must consequently have been viewed as of importance in the public mind. The passage relates to the power of making treaties; that of declaring war, being arranged with such obvious propriety among the legislative powers, as to be passed over without particular discussion.

"Tho' several writers on the subject of government place that power (*of making treaties*) in the class of *Executive authorities,* yet this is *evidently* an *arbitrary disposition.* For if we attend *carefully,* to its operation, it will be found to partake *more* of the *legislative* than of the *executive* character, though it does not seem strictly to fall within the definition of either of them. The essence of the legislative authority, is to enact laws; or in other words, to prescribe rules for the regulation of the society. While the execution of the laws and the employment of the common strength, either for this purpose, or for the common defence, seem to comprize *all* the functions of the *Executive magistrate.* The power of making treaties is *plainly* neither the one nor the other. It relates neither to the execution of the subsisting laws, nor to the enaction of new ones, and still less to an exertion of the common strength. Its objects are contracts with foreign nations, which have the *force of law,* but derive it from the obligations of good faith. They are not rules prescribed by the sovereign to the subject, but agreements between sovereign and sovereign. The power in question seems therefore to form a distinct department, and to belong properly neither to the legislative nor to the executive. The qualities elsewhere detailed as indispensable in the management of foreign *negociations,* point out the executive as the most fit agent in those transactions: whilst the vast importance of the trust, and the operation of treaties *as Laws,* plead strongly for the participation of the whole or a part of the *legislative body* in the office of making them." Federalist vol. 2. p. 273.[1]

It will not fail to be remarked on this commentary, that whatever doubts may be started as to the correctness of its reasoning against the legislative nature of the power to make treaties: it is *clear, consistent* and *confident,* in deciding that the power is *plainly* and *evidently* not an *executive power.*

HELVIDIUS

[1. *Federalist* 75.]

Madison claimed that Hamilton's construction of Washington's proc-
lamation as a neutrality proclamation constituted an infringement on
the legislative power, since a proclamation of neutrality might practi-
cally foreclose Congress's power to wage war or not. Congress always has
the right to declare war, but, he reasoned, the president's claim of the
right to judge national obligations under treaties could put Congress in
a position in which it would find it difficult to exercise its constitutional
rights. Article II does not determine the conduct of foreign relations.

Helvidius Number II

[31 August 1793]

The doctrine which has been examined, is pregnant with inferences and
consequences against which no ramparts in the constitution could defend
the public liberty, or scarcely the forms of Republican government. Were
it once established that the powers of war and treaty are in their nature
executive; that so far as they are not by strict construction transferred to the
legislature, they actually belong to the executive; that of course all powers
not less executive in their nature than those powers, if not granted to the
legislature may be claimed by the executive: if granted, are to be taken
strictly, with a residuary right in the executive; or, as will hereafter appear,
perhaps claimed as a concurrent right by the executive; and no citizen could
any longer guess at the character of the government under which he lives;
the most penetrating jurist would be unable to scan the extent of constructive prerogative.

Reprinted with permission from *The Papers of James Madison,* ed. Thomas A. Mason,
Robert A. Rutland, and Jeanne K. Sisson, vol. 15 (Charlottesville: University Press of Virginia, 1985), 80–87.

Leaving however to the leisure of the reader deductions which the author having omitted might not chuse to own, I proceed to the examination of one, with which that liberty cannot be taken.

"However true it may be (says he) that the right of the legislature to declare war *includes the right of judging* whether the legislature be under obligations to make war or not, it will not follow that the executive is *in any case* excluded from a *similar right* of judging in the execution of its own functions."

A material error of the writer in this application of his doctrine lies in his shrinking from its regular consequences. Had he stuck to his principle in its full extent, and reasoned from it without restraint, he would only have had to defend himself against his opponents. By yielding the great point, that the right to declare war, *tho' to be taken strictly,* includes the right to judge whether the nation be under obligation to make war or not, he is compelled to defend his argument not only against others but against himself also. Observe how he struggles in his own toils.

He had before admitted that the right to declare war is vested in the legislature. He here admits that the right to declare war includes the right to judge whether the United States be obliged to declare war or not. Can the inference be avoided, that the executive instead of having a similar right to judge, is as much excluded from the right to judge as from the right to declare?

If the right to declare war be an exception out of the general grant to the executive power; every thing included in the right must be included in the exception; and being included in the exception, is excluded from the grant.

He cannot disentangle himself by considering the right of the executive to judge as *concurrent* with that of the legislature. For if the executive have a concurrent right to judge, and the right to judge be included in (it is in fact the very essence of) the right to declare, he must go on and say that the executive has a concurrent right also to declare. And then what will he do with his other admission, that the power to declare is an exception out of the executive power.

Perhaps an attempt may be made to creep out of the difficulty through the words "in the execution of its functions." Here again he must equally fail.

Whatever difficulties may arise in defining the executive authority in particular cases, there can be none in deciding on an authority clearly placed by the constitution in another department. In this case the constitution has decided what shall not be deemed an executive authority; tho' it may not have clearly decided in every case what shall be so deemed. The declaring of war is expressly made a legislative function. The judging of the obligations to make war, is admitted to be included as a legislative function. Whenever then a question occurs whether war shall be declared, or whether public stipulations require it, the question necessarily belongs to the department to which these functions belong—And no other department can be *in the execution of its proper functions,* if it should undertake to decide such a question.

There can be no refuge against this conclusion, but in the pretext of a *concurrent* right in both departments to judge of the obligations to declare war, and this must be intended by the writer when he says, "it will not follow that the executive is excluded *in any case* from a *similar right* of judging &c."

As this is the ground on which the ultimate defence is to be made, and which must either be maintained, or the works erected on it, demolished; it will be proper to give its strength a fair trial.

It has been seen that the idea of a *concurrent* right is at variance with other ideas advanced or admitted by the writer. Laying aside for the present that consideration, it seems impossible to avoid concluding that if the executive has a concurrent right with the legislature to judge of obligations to declare war, and the right to judge be essentially included in the right to declare, it must have the same right to declare as it has to judge; & by another analogy, the same right to judge of other causes of war, as of the particular cause found in a public stipulation. So that whenever the executive *in the course of its functions* shall meet with these cases, it must either infer an equal authority in all, or acknowledge its want of authority in any.

If any doubt can remain, or rather if any doubt could ever have arisen, which side of the alternative ought to be embraced, it can be with those only who overlook or reject some of the most obvious and essential truths in political science.

The power to judge of the causes of war as involved in the power to declare war, is expressly vested where all other legislative powers are vested, that is, in the Congress of the United States. It is consequently determined by the constitution to be a *Legislative power.* Now omitting the enquiry here in what respects a compound power may be partly legislative, and partly executive, and accordingly vested *partly* in the one, and *partly* in the other department, or *jointly* in both; a remark used on another occasion is equally conclusive on this, that the same power, cannot belong *in the whole,* to *both* departments, or be properly so vested as to operate *separately* in *each.* Still more evident is it, that the same *specific function or act,* cannot possibly belong to the *two* departments and be *separately* exerciseable by *each.*

Legislative power may be *concurrently* vested in different legislative bodies. Executive powers may be concurrently vested in different executive magistrates. In legislative acts the executive may have a participation, as in the qualified negative on the laws. In executive acts, the legislature, or at least a branch of it, may participate, as in the appointment to offices. Arrangements of this sort are familiar in theory, as well as in practice. But an independent exercise of an *executive act,* by the legislature *alone,* or of a *legislative act* by the executive *alone,* one or other of which must happen in every case where the same act is exerciseable by each, and the latter of which would happen in the case urged by the writer, is contrary to one of the first and best maxims of a well organized government, and ought never to be founded in a forced construction, much less in opposition to a fair one. Instances, it is true, may be discovered among ourselves where this maxim, has not been faithfully pursued; but being generally acknowledged to be errors, they confirm, rather than impeach the truth and value of the maxim.

It may happen also that different independent departments, the legislative and executive, for example, may in the exercise of their functions, interpret the constitution differently, and thence lay claim each to the same power. This difference of opinion is an inconvenience not entirely to be avoided. It results from what may be called, if it be thought fit, a *concurrent* right to expound the constitution. But *this species* of concurrence is obviously and radically different from that in question. The former supposes the constitution to have given the power to one department only; and the doubt to be to which it has been given. The latter supposes it to belong to both; and that it may be exercised by either or both, according to the course of exigencies.

A concurrent authority in two independent departments to perform the same function with respect to the same thing, would be as awkward in practice, as it is unnatural in theory.

If the legislature and executive have both a right to judge of the obligations to make war or not, it must sometimes happen, though not at present, that they will judge differently. The executive may proceed to consider the question to-day, may determine that the United States are not bound to take part in a war, and *in the execution of its functions* proclaim that determination to all the world. To-morrow, the legislature may follow in the consideration of the same subject, may determine that the obligations impose war on the United States, and *in the execution of its functions,* enter into a *constitutional declaration,* expressly contradicting the *constitutional proclamation.*

In what light does this present the constitution to the people who established it? In what light would it present to the world, a nation, thus speaking, thro' two different organs, equally constitutional and authentic, two opposite languages, on the same subject and under the same existing circumstances?

But it is not with the legislative rights alone that this doctrine interferes. The rights of the judiciary may be equally invaded. For it is clear that if a right declared by the constitution to be legislative, and actually vested by it in the legislature, leaves, notwithstanding, a similar right in the executive whenever a case for exercising it occurs, *in the course of its functions:* a right declared to be judiciary and vested in that department may, on the same principle, be assumed and exercised by the executive *in the course of its functions:* and it is evident that occasions and pretexts for the latter interference may be as frequent as for the former. So again the judiciary department may find equal occasions in the execution of *its* functions, for usurping the authorities of the executive: and the legislature for stepping into the jurisdiction of both. And thus all the powers of government, of which a partition is so carefully made among the several branches, would be thrown into absolute hotchpot, and exposed to a general scramble.

It is time however for the writer himself to be heard, in defence of his text. His comment is in the words following:

"If the legislature have a right to make war on the one hand, it is on the other the duty of the executive to preserve peace, till war is declared; and in fulfilling that duty, it must necessarily possess a right of judging what is the nature of the obligations which the treaties of the country impose on the government; and when in pursuance of this right it has concluded that there is nothing inconsistent with a state of neutrality, it becomes both its province and its duty to enforce the laws incident to that state of the nation. The executive is charged with the execution of all laws, the laws of nations, as well as the municipal law which recognizes, and adopts those laws. It is consequently bound, by faithfully executing the laws of neutrality, when that is the state of the nation, to avoid giving a cause of war to foreign powers."

To do full justice to this master piece of logic, the reader must have the patience to follow it step by step.

If the legislature have a right to make war on the one hand, it is on the other, the duty of the executive to preserve peace till war is declared.

It will be observed that here is an explicit and peremptory assertion, that it is the *duty* of the executive *to preserve peace,* till *war is declared.*

And in fulfilling that duty it must necessarily possess a right of judging what is the nature of the obligations which the treaties of the country impose on the government: That is to say, in fulfilling *the duty to preserve peace,* it must necessarily possess the right to judge whether *peace ought to be preserved;* in other words *whether its duty should be performed.* Can words express a flatter contradiction? It is self evident that the *duty* in this case is so far from *necessarily implying the right,* that it *necessarily excludes it.*

And when in pursuance of this right it has concluded that there is nothing in them (obligations) inconsistent with a state of neutrality, IT BECOMES *both its province and its duty to enforce the laws incident to that state of the nation.*

70

And what if it should conclude that there is something inconsistent? Is it or is it not the province and duty of the executive to enforce the same laws? Say it is, you destroy the right to judge. Say it is not, you cancel the duty to obey.

Take this sentence in connection with the preceeding and the contradictions are multiplied. Take it by itself, and it makes the right to judge and conclude whether war be obligatory, absolute, and operative; and the duty to preserve peace, subordinate and conditional.

It will have been remarked by the attentive reader that the term *peace* in the first clause has been silently exchanged in the present one, for the term *neutrality*. Nothing however is gained by shifting the terms. Neutrality means peace; with an allusion to the circumstance of other nations being at war. The term has no reference to the existence or non-existence of treaties or alliances between the nation at peace and the nations at war. The laws incident to a state of neutrality, are the laws incident to a state of peace, with such circumstantial modifications only as are required by the new relation of the nations at war: Until war therefore be duly authorised by the United States they are as *actually* neutral when other nations are at war, as they are at peace, (if such a distinction in the terms is to be kept up) when other nations are not at war. The existence of *eventual* engagements which can only take effect on the declaration of the legislature, cannot, without that declaration, change the *actual* state of the country, any more in the eye of the executive than in the eye of the judiciary department. The laws to be the guide of both, remain the same to each, and the same to both.

Nor would more be gained by allowing the writer to define than to shift the term neutrality. For suppose, if you please, the existence of obligations to join in war to be inconsistent with neutrality, the question returns upon him, what laws are to be inforced by the executive until effect shall be given to those obligations by the declaration of the legislature? Are they to be the laws incident to those obligations, that is incident to war? However strongly the doctrines or deductions of the writer may tend to this point, it will not be avowed. Are the laws to be enforced by the executive, then, in such a state of things, to be the *same* as if no such obligations existed?

Admit this, which you must admit if you reject the other alternative, and the argument lands precisely where it embarked—in the position, that it is the absolute duty of the executive in all cases to preserve peace till war is declared, not that it is "*to become* the province and duty of the executive" after it has concluded that there is nothing in those obligations inconsistent with a state of peace and neutrality. The right to judge and conclude therefore so solemnly maintained in the text is lost in the comment.

We shall see whether it can be reinstated by what follows—

The executive is charged with the execution of all laws, the laws of nations as well as the municipal law which recognizes and adopts those laws. It is consequently bound, by faithfully executing the laws of neutrality when that is the state of the nation, to avoid giving cause of war to foreign powers.

The first sentence is a truth, but nothing to the point in question. The last is *partly true* in its proper meaning, but *totally untrue* in the meaning of the writer. That the executive is bound faithfully to execute the laws of neutrality, whilst those laws continue unaltered by the competent authority, is true; but not for the reason here given, to wit, to avoid giving cause of war to foreign powers. It is bound to the faithful execution of these as of all other laws internal and external, by the nature of its trust and the sanction of its oath, even if turbulent citizens should consider its so doing as a cause of war at home, or unfriendly nations should consider its so doing, as a cause of war abroad. The duty of the executive to preserve external peace, can no more suspend the force of external laws, than its duty to preserve internal peace can suspend the force of municipal laws.

It is certain that a faithful execution of the laws of neutrality may tend as much in some cases, to incur war from one quarter, as in others to avoid war from other quarters. The executive must nevertheless execute the laws of neutrality whilst in force, and leave it to the legislature to decide whether they ought to be altered or not. The executive has no other discretion than to convene and give information to the legislature on occasions that may demand it; and whilst this discretion is duly exercised the trust of the executive is satisfied, and that department is not responsible for the consequences. It could not be made responsible for them without vesting it with the legislative as well as with the executive trust.

These remarks are obvious and conclusive, on the supposition that the expression "laws of neutrality" means simply what the words import, and what alone they can mean, to give force or colour to the inference of the writer from his own premises. As the inference itself however in its proper meaning, does not approach towards his avowed object, which is to work out a prerogative for the executive to judge, in common with the legislature, whether there be cause of war or not in a public obligation, it is to be presumed that "in faithfully executing the laws of neutrality" an exercise of that prerogative was meant to be included. On this supposition the inference, as will have been seen, does not result from his own premises, and has been already so amply discussed, and, it is conceived, so clearly disproved, that not a word more can be necessary on this branch of his argument.

HELVIDIUS

Madison argues that the authority of the executive to receive ambassa-
dors and other public ministers does not extend to the question whether
an existing government ought to be recognized or not, and furthermore
that a change in the government cannot be used to justify the right to
refuse or receive ambassadors and other public ministers.

Helvidius Number III

[7 September 1793]

In order to give color to a right in the Executive to exercise the Legislative power of judging whether there be a cause of war in a public stipulation—two other arguments are subjoined by the writer to that last examined.

The first is simply this, "It is the right and duty of the Executive to judge of and interpret those articles of our treaties which give to France particular privileges, *in order to the enforcement of those privileges,*" from which it is stated as a necessary consequence, that the Executive has certain other rights, among which is the right in question.

This argument is answered by a very obvious distinction. The first right is essential to the execution of the treaty *as a law in operation,* and interferes with no right invested in another Department. The second is not essential to the execution of the treaty or any other law; on the contrary the article to which the right is applied, cannot as has been shewn, from the very nature of it be *in operation* as a law without a previous declaration of the Legislature; and all the laws to be enforced by the Executive remain in the mean time precisely the same, whatever be the disposition or judgment of the

Reprinted with permission from *The Papers of James Madison,* ed. Thomas A. Mason, Robert A. Rutland, and Jeanne K. Sisson, vol. 15 (Charlottesville: University Press of Virginia, 1985), 95–103.

Executive. This second right would also interfere with a right acknowledged to be in the Legislative Department.

If nothing else could suggest this distinction to the writer, he ought to have been reminded of it by his own words "in order to the enforcement of those privileges"—was it in order to *the enforcement* of the article of guaranty, that the right is ascribed to the Executive?

The other of the two arguments reduces itself into the following form: The Executive has the right to receive public Ministers; this right includes the right of deciding, in the case of a revolution, whether the new government sending the Minister, ought to be recognized or not; and this again, the right to give or refuse operation to pre-existing treaties.

The power of the Legislature to declare war and judge of the causes for declaring it, is one of the most express and explicit parts of the Constitution. To endeavor to abridge or *effect it* by strained inferences, and by hypothetical or singular occurrences, naturally warns the reader of some lurking fallacy.

The words of the Constitution are "he (the President) shall receive Ambassadors, other public Ministers and Consuls." I shall not undertake to examine what would be the precise extent and effect of this function in various cases which fancy may suggest, or which time may produce. It will be more proper to observe in general, and every candid reader will second the observation, that little if any thing more was intended by the clause, than to provide for a particular mode of communication, *almost* grown into a right among modern nations; by pointing out the department of the government, most proper for the ceremony of admitting public Ministers, of examining their credentials, and of authenticating their title to the privileges annexed to their character by the law of nations. This being the apparent design of the Constitution, it would be highly improper to magnify the function into an important prerogative, even where no rights of other departments could be affected by it.

To shew that the view here given of the clause is not a new construction, invented or strained for a particular occasion—I will take the liberty of recurring to the cotemporary work already quoted, which contains the obvious and original gloss put on this part of the Constitution by its friends and advocates.

"The President is also to be authorised to receive Ambassadors and other public Ministers. This, though it has been a rich theme of declamation, is more a matter of *dignity* than of *authority*. It is a circumstance, that will be *without consequence* in the administration of the government, and it is far more convenient that it should be arranged in this manner, than that there should be a necessity for convening the Legislature or one of its branches upon every arrival of a foreign Minister, though it were merely to take the place of a departed predecessor." Fed. vol. II. p. 237.[1]

Had it been foretold in the year 1788 when this work was published, that before the end of the year 1793, a writer, assuming the merit of being a friend to the Constitution, would appear, and gravely maintain, that this function, which was to be *without consequence* in the administration of the government, might have the consequence of deciding on the validity of revolutions in favor of liberty, "of putting the United States in a condition to become an associate in war," nay "of laying the *Legislature* under an *obligation* of *declaring* war," what would have been thought and said of so visionary a prophet?

The moderate opponents of the Constitution would probably have disowned his extravagance. By the advocates of the Constitution, his prediction must have been treated as "an experiment on public credulity, dictated either by a deliberate intention to deceive, or by the overflowings of a zeal too intemperate to be ingenuous."[2]

But how does it follow from the function to receive Ambassadors and other public Ministers that so consequential a prerogative may be exercised by the Executive? When a foreign Minister presents himself, two questions immediately arise: Are his credentials from the existing and acting government of his country? Are they properly authenticated? These questions belong of necessity to the Executive; but they involve no cognizance of the question, whether those exercising the government have the right along

[1. *Federalist* 69.]
[2. *Federalist* 24.]

with the possession. This belongs to the nation, and to the nation alone, on whom the government operates. The questions before the Executive are merely questions of fact; and the Executive would have precisely the same right, or rather be under the same necessity of deciding them, if its function was simply to receive *without any discretion to reject* public Ministers. It is evident, therefore, that if the Executive has a right to reject a public Minister it must be founded on some other consideration than a change in the government or the newness of the government; and consequently a right to refuse to acknowledge a new government cannot be implied by the right to refuse a public Minister.

It is not denied that there may be cases in which a respect to the general principles of liberty, the essential rights of the people, or the over-ruling sentiments of humanity, might require a government, whether new or old, to be treated as an illegitimate despotism. Such are in fact discussed and admitted by the most approved authorities. But they are great and extraordinary cases, by no means submitted to so limited an organ of the national will as the Executive of the United States; and certainly not to be brought, by any torture of words, within the right to receive Ambassadors.

That the authority of the Executive does not extend to question, whether an existing government ought to be recognized or not, will still more clearly appear from an examination of the next inference of the writer, to wit, that the Executive has a right to give or refuse activity and operation to pre-existing treaties.

If there be a principle that ought not to be questioned within the United States, it is, that every nation has a right to abolish an old government and establish a new one. This principle is not only recorded in every public archive, written in every American heart, and sealed with the blood of a host of American martyrs; but is the only lawful tenure by which the United States hold their existence as a nation.

It is a principle incorporated with the above, that governments are established for the national good and are organs of the national will.

From these two principles results a third, that treaties formed by the government, are treaties of the nation, unless otherwise expressed in the treaties.

Another consequence is that a nation, by exercising the right of changing the organ of its will, can neither disengage itself from the obligations, nor forfeit the benefits of its treaties. This is a truth of vast importance, and happily rests with sufficient firmness on its own authority. To silence or prevent cavil, I insert however, the following extracts:

"Since then such a treaty (a treaty not *personal* to the sovereign) directly relates to the body of the State, it subsists though the form of the republic happens to be changed, and though it should be even transformed into a monarchy—For the State and the nation are always the same whatever changes are made in the form of the government—and the treaty concluded with the nation, remains in force as long as the nation exists." Vattel, B. II. § 185.[3]

"It follows that as a treaty, notwithstanding the change of a democratic government into a monarchy, continues in force with the new King, in like manner; if a *monarchy* becomes a *republic,* the treaty made with the King does not expire on that account, unless it was manifestly personal." Burlam. part IV, c. IX, § 16. ¶ 6.[4]

As a change of government then makes no change in the obligations or rights of the party to a treaty, it is clear that the Executive can have no more right to suspend or prevent the operation of a treaty, on account of the change, than to suspend or prevent the operation, where no such change has happened. Nor can it have any more right to suspend the operation of a treaty in force as a law, than to suspend the operation of any other law.

The logic employed by the writer on this occasion, will be best understood by accommodating to it the language of a proclamation, founded on the prerogative and policy of suspending the treaty with France.

Whereas a treaty was concluded on the   day of   between the United States and the French nation, through the kingly government, which was then the organ of its will: And whereas the said nation hath since exercised its right (no wise abridged by the said treaty) of changing the

[3. Vattel, *Law of Nations.*]
[4. Burlamaqui, *Principes du droit politique.*]

organ of its will, by abolishing the said kingly government, as inconsistent with the rights and happiness of the people, and establishing a republican in lieu thereof, as most favorable to the public happiness, and best suited to the genius of a people become sensible of their rights and ashamed of their chains: And whereas, by the constitution of the United States, the executive is authorised to receive ambassadors, other public ministers and consuls: And whereas a public minister, duly appointed and commissioned by the new Republic of France, hath arrived and presented himself to the executive, in order to be received in his proper character: Now be it known, that by virtue of the said right vested in the executive to receive ambassadors, other public ministers and consuls, & of the rights included therein, the executive hath refused to receive the said minister from the said republic, and hath thereby caused the activity and operation of all treaties with the French nation, *hitherto in force as supreme laws of the land,* to be suspended until the executive, by taking off the said suspension, shall revive the same; of which, all persons concerned are to take notice, at their peril.

The writer, as if beginning to feel that he was grasping at more than he could hold, endeavours, all of a sudden, to squeeze his doctrine into a smaller size, and a less vulnerable shape. The reader shall see the operation in his own words.

"And where *a treaty* antecedently exists between the United States and such nation (a nation whose government has undergone a revolution) that right (the right of judging whether the new rulers ought to be recognized or not) involves the power of giving operation or not to *such treaty. For* until the new government is acknowledged, the treaties between the nations, *as far at least* as regards *public rights,* are *of course* suspended."

This qualification of the suspending power, though reluctantly and inexplicitly made, was prudent, for two reasons; first, because it is pretty evident that *private rights,* whether of judiciary or executive cognizance, may be carried into effect without the agency of the foreign government; and therefore would not be suspended of course by a rejection of that agency. Secondly, because the judiciary, being an independent department, and acting under an oath to pursue the law of treaties as the supreme law of the land, might not readily follow the executive example, and a *right* in *one expositor* of treaties, to consider them as *not in force,* whilst it would be the *duty* of *another expositor* to consider them as *in force,* would be a phaenomenon not so easy to be explained. Indeed as the doctrine stands qualified, it leaves the executive the right of suspending the law of treaties in relation to rights of one description, without exempting it from the duty of enforcing it in relation to rights of another description.

But the writer is embarked in so unsound an argument, that he does not save the rest of his inference by this sacrifice of one half of it. It is not true, that *all public rights* are of course suspended by a refusal to acknowledge the government, or even by a suspension of the government. And in the next place, the right in question does not follow from the necessary suspension of public rights, in consequence of a refusal to acknowledge the government.

Public rights are of two sorts; those which require the agency of government; those which may be carried into effect without that agency.

As public rights are the rights of the nation, not of the government, it is clear that wherever they can be made good to the nation, without the office of government, they are not suspended by the want of an acknowledged government, or even by the want of an existing government; and that there are important rights of this description, will be illustrated by the following case:

Suppose, that after the conclusion of the treaty of alliance between the United States and France, a party of the enemy had surprised and put to death every member of congress; that the occasion had been used by the people of America for changing the old confederacy into such a government as now exists, and that in the progress of this revolution, an interregnum had happened. Suppose further, that during this interval, the states of South-Carolina and Georgia, or any other parts of the United States, had been attacked and been put into evident and imminent danger of being irrecoverably lost, without the interposition of the French arms; is it not manifest, that as the Treaty is the Treaty of the United States, not of their government, the people of the United States could not forfeit their right to the guarantee of their territory by the accidental suspension of their government; and that any attempt, on the part of France, to evade the obligations of the Treaty, by pleading the suspension of government, or by refusing to acknowledge it, would justly have been received with universal indignation, as an ignominious perfidy?

With respect to public rights that cannot take effect in favour of a nation without the agency of its government, it is admitted that they are suspended of course where there is no government in existence, and also by a refusal to acknowledge an existing government. But no inference in favour of *a right* to suspend the operation of Treaties, can be drawn from either case. Where the existence of the government is suspended, it is a case of necessity; it would be a case happening without the act of the executive, and consequently could prove nothing for or against the right.

In the other case, to wit, of a refusal by the executive to recognize an *existing government,* however certain it may be, that a suspension of some of the public rights might ensue, yet it is equally certain, that the refusal would be without right or authority; and that no right or authority could be implied or produced by the unauthorised act. If a right to do whatever might bear an analogy to the necessary consequence of what was done without right, could be inferred from the analogy, there would be no other limit to power than the limit to its ingenuity.

It is no answer to say that it may be doubtful whether a government does or does not exist; or doubtful which may be the existing and acting Government. The case stated by the writer is, that there are existing rulers; that there is an acting Government; but that they are *new* rulers; and that it is a *new* Government. The full reply, however, is to repeat what has been already observed; that questions of this sort are mere questions of fact; that as such only, they belong to the executive; that they would equally belong to the executive, if it was tied down to the reception of public ministers, without any discretion to receive or reject them; that where the fact appears to be, that no Government exists, the consequential suspension is independent of the executive; that where the fact appears to be, that the Government does exist, the executive must be governed by the fact, and can have no right or discretion, on account of the date or form of the Government, to refuse to acknowledge it, either by rejecting its public minister, or by any other step taken on that account. If it does refuse on that account, the refusal is a wrongful act, and can neither prove nor illustrate a rightful power.

I have spent more time on this part of the discussion than may appear to some, to have been requisite. But it was considered as a proper opportunity for presenting some important ideas, connected with the general subject, and it may be of use in shewing how very superficially, as well as erroneously, the writer has treated it.

In other respects so particular an investigation was less necessary. For allowing it to be, as contended, that a suspension of treaties might happen from a *consequential* operation of a right to receive public ministers, which is an *express right* vested by the constitution; it could be no proof, that the same or a *similar* effect could be produced by the *direct* operation of a *constructive power.*

Hence the embarrassments and gross contradictions of the writer in defining, and applying his ultimate inference from the operation of the executive power with regard to public ministers.

At first it exhibits an "important instance of the right of the executive to decide the obligation of the nation with regard to foreign nations."

Rising from that, it confers on the executive, a right "to put the United States in a condition to become an associate in war."

And, at its full height authorises the executive "to lay the legislature under *an obligation* of declaring war."

From this towering prerogative, it suddenly brings down the executive to the right of "*consequentially affecting* the proper or improper exercise of the power of the legislature to declare war."

And then, by a caprice as unexpected as it is sudden, it espouses the cause of the legislature; rescues it from the executive right "to lay it under an *obligation* of declaring war"; and asserts it to be "*free* to perform its *own* duties, according to its *own* sense of them," without any other controul than what it is liable to, in every other legislative act.

The point at which it finally seems to rest, is, that "the executive in the exercise of its *constitutional powers,* may establish an antecedent state of things, which ought to *weigh* in the *legislative decisions*"; a prerogative which will import a great deal, or nothing, according to the handle by which you take it; and which, at the same time, you can take by no handle that does not clash with some inference preceding.

If "by weighing in the legislative decisions" be meant having *an influence* on the *expediency* of this or that decision in the *opinion* of the legislature; this is no more than what every antecedent state of things ought to have, from whatever cause proceeding; whether from the use or abuse of constitutional powers, or from the exercise of constitutional or assumed powers. In this sense the power to establish an antecedent state of things is not constituted. But then it is of no use to the writer, and is also in direct contradiction to the inference, that the executive may "lay the *legislature* under an *obligation* to decide in favor of *war*."

If the meaning be as is implied by the force of the terms "constitutional powers" that the antecedent state of things produced by the executive, ought to have a *constitutional weight* with the legislature: or, in plainer words, imposes a *constitutional obligation* on the *legislative decisions,* the writer will not only have to combat the arguments by which such a prerogative has been disproved: but to reconcile it with his last concession, that "the legislature is *free* to perform its duties according to its *own* sense of them." He must shew that the legislature is, at the same time, *constitutionally free* to pursue its *own judgment* and *constitutionally bound* by the *judgment of the executive.*

HELVIDIUS

Madison continues the discussion of the doctrine that the powers of treaty and war are by nature executive powers. Here he argues that this doctrine introduces new principles into the Constitution and works to remove the landmarks of power by giving to the executive the prerogative of judging and deciding whether there are causes of war or not in the obligations of treaties.

Helvidius Number IV

[14 September 1793]

The last papers compleated the view proposed to be taken of the arguments in support of the new and aspiring doctrine, which ascribes to the executive the prerogative of judging and deciding whether there be causes of war or not, in the obligations of treaties; notwithstanding the express provision in the constitution, by which the legislature is made the organ of the national will, on questions whether there be or be not a cause for declaring war. If the answer to these arguments has imparted the conviction which dictated it, the reader will have pronounced, that they are generally superficial, abounding in contradictions, never in the least degree conclusive to the main point, and not unfrequently conclusive against the writer himself: whilst the doctrine—that the powers of treaty and war, are in their nature executive powers—which forms the basis of those arguments, is as indefensible and as dangerous, as the particular doctrine to which they are applied.

But it is not to be forgotten that these doctrines, though ever so clearly disproved, or ever so weakly defended, remain before the public a striking

Reprinted with permission from *The Papers of James Madison,* ed. Thomas A. Mason, Robert A. Rutland, and Jeanne K. Sisson, vol. 15 (Charlottesville: University Press of Virginia, 1985), 106–10.

monument of the principles and views which are entertained and propagated in the community.

It is also to be remembered, that however the consequences flowing from such premises, may be disavowed at this time or by this individual, we are to regard it as morally certain, that in proportion as the doctrines make their way into the creed of the government, and the acquiescence of the public, every power that can be deduced from them, will be deduced and exercised sooner or later by those who may have an interest in so doing. The character of human nature gives this salutary warning to every sober and reflecting mind. And the history of government, in all its forms and in every period of time, ratifies the danger. A people therefore, who are so happy as to possess the inestimable blessing of a free and defined constitution, cannot be too watchful against the introduction, nor too critical in tracing the consequences, of new principles and new constructions, that may remove the landmarks of power.

Should the prerogative which has been examined, be allowed in its most limited sense, to usurp the public countenance, the interval would probably be very short, before it would be heard from some quarter or other, that the prerogative either amounts to nothing, or means a right to judge and conclude that the obligations of treaty impose war, as well as that they permit peace. That it is fair reasoning, to say, that if the prerogative exists at all, an *operative* rather than an *inert* character ought to be given to it.

In support of this conclusion, there would be enough to echo, ⟨"that the prerogative in this active sense, is connected with the executive⟩ in various capacities—as the organ of intercourse between the nation and foreign nations—as the interpreter of national treaties" (a violation of which may be a cause of war) "as that power which is charged with the execution of the laws of which treaties make a part—as that power, which is charged with *the command and application of the public force.*"

With additional force, it might be said, that the executive is as much the *executor* as the *interpreter* of treaties: that if by virtue of the *first* character it is to judge of the *obligations* of treaties, it is by virtue of the *second*, equally authorised to carry those obligations *into effect*. Should there occur for example, a *casus federis,* claiming a military co-operation of the United States, and a military force should happen to be under the command of the executive, it must have the same right, as *executor of public treaties* to *employ* the public force, as it has in quality of *interpreter of public treaties* to decide whether it ought to be *employed.*

The case of a treaty of peace would be an auxiliary to comments of this sort. It is a condition annexed to every treaty that an infraction even of an important article, on one side extinguishes the obligations on the other: and the immediate consequence of a dissolution of a treaty of peace is a restoration of a state of war. If the executive is "to decide on the obligation of the nation with regard to foreign nations"—"to pronounce the *existing condition* (in the sense annexed by the writer) of the nation with regard to them; and to admonish the citizens of their obligations and duties as founded upon *that condition* of things"—"to judge what are the *reciprocal rights* and obligations of the United States, and of all and each of the powers at war:"—add, that if the executive moreover possesses all powers relating to war *not strictly* within the power *to declare war,* which any pupil of political casuistry, could distinguish from a mere *relapse* into a war, that *had been declared:* With this store of materials and the example given of the use to be made of them, would it be difficult to fabricate a power in the executive to plunge the nation into war, whenever a treaty of peace might happen to be infringed?

But if any difficulty should arise, there is another mode chalked out by which the end might clearly be brought about, even without the violation of the treaty of peace; especially if the other party should happen to change its government at the crisis. The executive, in that case, could *suspend* the treaty of peace *by refusing to receive an ambassador* from the *new* government, and the state of war *emerges of course.*

This is a sample of the use to which the extraordinary publication we are reviewing, might be turned. Some of the inferences could not be repelled at all. And the least regular of them must go smoothly down with those, who had swallowed the gross sophistry which wrapped up the original dose.

Every just view that can be taken of this subject, admonishes the public, of the necessity of a rigid adherence to the simple, the received and the fundamental doctrine of the constitution, that the power to declare war including the power of judging of the causes of war is *fully* and *exclusively* vested in the legislature: that the executive has no right, in any case to decide the question, whether there is or is not cause for declaring war: that the right of convening and informing Congress, whenever such a question seems to call for a decision, is all the right which the constitution has deemed requisite or proper: and that for such more than for any other contingency, this right was specially given to the executive.

In no part of the constitution is more wisdom to be found than in the clause which confides the question of war or peace to the legislature, and not to the executive department. Beside the objection to such a mixture of heterogeneous powers: the trust and the temptation would be too great for any one man: not such as nature may offer as the prodigy of many centuries, but such as may be expected in the ordinary successions of magistracy. War is in fact the true nurse of executive aggrandizement. In war a physical force is to be created, and it is the executive will which is to direct it. In war the public treasures are to be unlocked, and it is the executive hand which is to dispense them. In war the honors and emoluments of office are to be multiplied; and it is the executive patronage under which they are to be enjoyed. It is in war, finally, that laurels are to be gathered, and it is the executive brow they are to encircle. The strongest passions, and most dangerous weaknesses of the human breast; ambition, avarice, vanity, the honorable or venial love of fame, are all in conspiracy against the desire and duty of peace.

Hence it has grown into an axiom that the executive is the department of power most distinguished by its propensity to war: hence it is the practice of all states, in proportion as they are free, to disarm this propensity of its influence.

As the best praise then that can be pronounced on an executive magistrate, is, that he is the friend of peace; a praise that rises in its value, as there may be a known capacity to shine in war: so it must be one of the most sacred duties of a free people, to mark the first omen in the society, of principles that may stimulate the hopes of other magistrates of another propensity, to intrude into questions on which its gratification depends. If a free people be a wise people also, they will not forget that the danger of surprise can never be so great, as when the advocates for the prerogative of war, can sheathe it in a symbol of peace.

The constitution has manifested a similar prudence in refusing to the executive the *sole* power of making peace. The trust in this instance also, would be too great for the wisdom, and the temptations too strong for the virtue, of a single citizen. The principal reasons on which the constitution proceeded in its regulation of the power of treaties, including treaties of peace, are so aptly furnished by the work already quoted more than once, that I shall borrow another comment from that source.

"However proper or safe it may be in a government where the executive magistrate is an hereditary monarch to commit to him the entire power of making treaties, it would be utterly unsafe and improper to entrust that power to an elective magistrate of four years duration. It has been remarked upon another occasion, and the remark is unquestionably just, that an hereditary monarch, though often the oppressor of his people, has personally too much at stake in the government to be in any material danger of being corrupted by foreign powers. But that a man raised from the station of a private citizen to the rank of chief magistrate, possessed of but a moderate or slender fortune, and looking forward to a period not very remote, when he may probably be obliged to return to the station from which he was taken, might sometimes be under temptations to sacrifice his duty to his interest, which it would require superlative virtue to withstand. An avaricious man might be tempted to betray the interests of the state to the acquisition of wealth. An ambitious man might make his own aggrandizement, by the aid of a foreign power, the price of his treachery to his constituents. The history of human conduct does not warrant that exalted opinion of human virtue, which would make it wise in a nation, to commit interests of so delicate and momentous a kind as *those which concern its intercourse* with the rest of the world, to the *sole* disposal of a magistrate, created and circumstanced, as would be a President of the United States."[1]

[1. *Federalist* 75.]

I shall conclude this paper and this branch of the subject, with two reflections, which naturally arise from this view of the Constitution.

The first is, that as the personal interest of an hereditary monarch in the government, is the *only* security against the temptation incident to a commitment of the delicate and momentous interests of the nation which concern its intercourse with the rest of the world, to the disposal of a single magistrate, it is a plain consequence, that every addition that may be made to the *sole* agency and influence of the Executive, in the intercourse of the nation with foreign nations, is an increase of the dangerous temptation to which an *elective and temporary* magistrate is exposed; and an *argument* and *advance* towards the security afforded by the personal interests of an *hereditary* magistrate.

Secondly, As the constitution has not permitted the Executive *singly* to conclude or judge that peace ought to be made, it might be inferred from that circumstance alone, that it never meant to give it authority, *singly*, to judge and conclude that war ought not to be made. The trust would be precisely similar and equivalent in the two cases. The right to say that war ought not to go on, would be no greater than the right to say that war ought to begin. Every danger of error or corruption, incident to such a prerogative in one case, is incident to it in the other. If the Constitution therefore has deemed it unsafe or improper in the one case, it must be deemed equally so in the other case.

HELVIDIUS

Madison discusses the dangerous implications in a neutrality proclamation of representing the executive as having the constitutional right to interfere with any question of a cause of war.

Helvidius Number V

[18 September 1793]

Having seen that the executive has no constitutional right to interfere in any question whether there be or be not a cause of war, and the extensive consequences flowing from the doctrines on which a claim has been asserted, it remains to be enquired whether the writer is better warranted in the fact which he assumes, namely that the proclamation of the Executive has undertaken to decide the question, whether there be a cause of war or not, in the article of guaranty between the United States and France, and, in so doing has exercised the right which is claimed for that department.

Before I proceed to the examination of this point, it may not be amiss to advert to the novelty of the phraseology, as well as of the doctrines, expounded by this writer. The source from which the former is evidently borrowed, may enlighten our conjectures with regard to the source of the latter. It is a just observation also that words have often a gradual influence on ideas, and when used in an improper sense, may cover fallacies which would not otherwise escape detection.

I allude particularly to his application of the term *government* to the *Executive authority alone.* The Proclamation is "a manifestation of the sense of the *government*"; "why did not the *government* wait, &c." "The policy on

Reprinted with permission from *The Papers of James Madison,* ed. Thomas A. Mason, Robert A. Rutland, and Jeanne K. Sisson, vol. 15 (Charlottesville: University Press of Virginia, 1985), 113–20.

the part of the *government* of removing all doubt as to *its own disposition.*"*
"It was of great importance that our citizens should understand as early as
possible the opinion entertained by the *government, &c.*" If in addition to
the rest, the early manifestation of *the views* of the *government,* had any effect *in fixing the public opinion, &c.* The reader will probably be struck with
the reflection, that if the Proclamation really possessed the character, and
was to have the effects, here ascribed to it, something more than the authority of *the government,* in the writer's sense of government, would have
been a necessary sanction to the act, and if the term "government" be re-
moved, and that of "President" substituted, in the sentences quoted, the
justice of the reflection will be felt with peculiar force. But I remark only,
on the singularity of the stile adopted by the writer, as shewing either that
the phraseology of a foreign government is more familiar to him than the
phraseology proper to our own, or that he wishes to propagate a familiar-
ity of the former in preference to the latter. I do not know what degree of
disapprobation others may think due to this innovation of language, but I
consider it as far above a trivial criticism, to observe that it is by no means
unworthy of attention, whether viewed with an eye to its probable cause
or its apparent tendency, "the government," unquestionably means in the
United States the whole government, not the executive part, either exclusively, or *pre-eminently;* as it may do in a monarchy, where the splendor of
prerogative eclipses, and the machinery of influence, directs, every other
part of the government. In the former and proper sense, the term has hitherto been used in official proceedings, in public discussions, and in private
discourse. It is as short and as easy, and less liable to misapprehension, to
say, the Executive or the President, as to say the government. In a word the
new dialect could not proceed either from necessity, conveniency, propriety, or perspicuity; and being in opposition to common usage, so marked a
fondness for it, justifies the notice here taken of it. It shall no longer detain
me, however, from the more important subject of the present paper.

---

* *The writer ought not in the same paper, No. VII, to have said, "Had the President announced his own disposition, he would have been chargeable with egotism, if not presumption."*

I proceed therefore to observe that as a "Proclamation," in its *ordinary* use, is an address to citizens or subjects only; as it is always understood to relate to the law *actually in operation,* and to be an act *purely* and *exclusively* Executive; there can be no implication in the *name* or the *form* of such an instrument, that it was meant *principally,* for the information of foreign nations; far less that it related to an *eventual stipulation* on a subject, *acknowledged* to be within the *Legislative province.*

When the writer therefore undertook to engraft his new prerogative on the Proclamation by ascribing to it so unusual, and unimplied a meaning, it was evidently incumbent on him to shew, that the *text* of the instrument could not be satisfied by any other construction than his own. Has he done this? No. What has he done? He has called the Proclamation a Proclamation of neutrality; he has put his own arbitrary meaning on that phrase, and has then proceeded in his arguments and his inferences, with as much confidence, as if no question was ever to be asked, whether the term "neutrality" be in the Proclamation; or whether, if there, it could justify the use he makes of it.

It has appeared from observations already made, that if the term "neutrality" was in the Proclamation, it could not avail the writer, in the present discussion; but the fact is no such term is to be found in it, nor any other term, of a meaning equivalent to that, in which the term neutrality is used by him.

There is the less pretext, in the present case, for hunting after any latent or extraordinary object because an obvious and legal one, is at hand, to satisfy the occasion on which the Proclamation issued. The existence of war among several nations with which the United States have an extensive intercourse; the duty of the Executive to preserve peace by enforcing its laws, whilst those laws continued in force; the danger that indiscreet citizens might be tempted or surprised by the crisis, into unlawful proceedings, tending to involve the United States in a war, which the competent authority might decide them to be at liberty to avoid, and which, if they should be judged not at liberty to avoid, the other party to the *eventual contract,* might not be willing to impose on them; these surely might have been sufficient grounds for the measure pursued by the executive, and being legal and rational grounds, it would be wrong, if there be no necessity, to look beyond them.

If there be any thing in the Proclamation of which the writer could have made a handle, it is the part which declares, the *disposition,* the *duty* and the *interest* of the United States, in relation to the war existing in Europe. As the Legislature is the only competent and constitutional organ of the will of the nation; that is, of its disposition, its duty and its interest, in relation to a commencement of war, in like manner as the President and Senate *jointly,* not the President *alone,* are in relation to peace, after war has been commenced—I will not dissemble my wish that a language less exposed to criticism had been preferred; but taking the expressions, in the sense of the writer himself, as analogous to the language which might be proper, on the reception of a public Minister, or any similar occasion, it is evident, that his construction can derive no succour, even from this resource.

If the Proclamation then does not *require* the construction which this writer has taken the liberty of putting on it; I leave it to be decided whether the following considerations do not forbid us to suppose, that the President could have intended, by that act, to embrace and prejudge the Legislative question whether there was, or was not, under the circumstances of the case, a cause of war in the article of guaranty.

It has been shewn that such an intention would have usurped a prerogative not vested in the Executive, and even *confessedly* vested in another department.

In exercising the Constitutional power of deciding a question of war, the Legislature ought to be as free to decide, according to its own sense of the public good, on one side as on the other side. Had the Proclamation prejudged the question on either side, and *proclaimed its decision to the world;* the Legislature, instead of being as free as it ought, might be thrown under the dilemma, of either sacrificing its judgment to that of the Executive; or by opposing the Executive judgment, of producing a relation between the two departments, extremely delicate among ourselves, and of the worst influence on the national character and interests abroad; a variance of this nature, it will readily be perceived, would be very different from a want of conformity to the *mere recommendations* of the Executive, in the measures adopted by the Legislature.

It does not appear that such a Proclamation could have even pleaded any call, from either of the parties at war with France, for an explanation of the light in which the guaranty was viewed—whilst, indeed, no positive indication whatever was given of hostile purposes, it is not conceived, that any power could have decently made such an application—or if they had, that a Proclamation, would have been either a satisfactory, or an honorable answer. It could not have been satisfactory, if serious apprehensions were entertained, because it would not have proceeded from that authority which alone could definitely pronounce the will of the United States on the subject. It would not have been honorable, because a private diplomatic answer only is due to a private diplomatic application; and to have done so much more, would have marked a pusilanimity and want of dignity in the Executive Magistrate.

But whether the Executive was or was not applied to, or whatever weight be allowed to that circumstance, it ought never to be presumed, that the Executive would so abruptly, so publicly, and so solemnly, proceed to disclaim a sense of the contract, which the other party might consider and wish to support by discussion as its true and reasonable import. It is asked, indeed, in a tone that sufficiently displays the spirit in which the writer construes both the Proclamation and the treaty, "Did the Executive stand in need of the logic of a foreign agent to enlighten it as to the duties or the interests of the nation; or was it bound to ask his consent to a step which appeared to itself consistent with the former, and conducive to the latter? The sense of treaties was to be learnt from the treaties themselves." Had he consulted his Vattel, instead of his animosity to France, he would have discovered that however humiliating it might be to wait for a foreign logic, to assist the interpretation of an act depending on the national authority alone, yet in the case of a treaty, which is as much the treaty of a foreign nation, as it is ours; and in which foreign duties and rights are as much involved as ours, the sense of the treaty, though to be learnt from the treaty itself, is to be equally learned by both parties to it. Neither of them can have a right more than the other, to say what a particular article means; and where there is equality without a judge consultation is as consistent with dignity as it is conducive to harmony and friendship, let Vattel however be heard on the subject.

"The third general maxim, or principle, on the subject of interpretation (of Treaties) is: *'That neither the one nor the other of the interested or contracting powers has a right to interpret the act or treaty at its pleasure.* For if you are at liberty to give my promise what sense you please, you will have the power of obliging me to do whatever you have a mind, contrary to my intention, and beyond my real engagement: and reciprocally, *if I am allowed to explain my promises as I please, I may render them vain and illusive, by giving them a sense quite different from that in which they were presented to you, and in which you must have taken them in accepting them.'*" Vat. B. II. c. vii. §. 265.[1]

The writer ought to have been particularly sensible of the improbability that a precipitate and *ex parte* decision of the question arising under the guaranty, could have been intended by the proclamation. He had but just gone through his undertaking, to prove that the article of guaranty like the rest of the treaty is defensive, not offensive. He had examined his books and retailed his quotations, to shew that the criterion between the two kinds of war is the circumstance of priority in the attack. He could not therefore but know, that according to his own principles, the question whether the United States, were under an obligation or not to take part in the war, was a *question of fact* whether the first attack was made by France or her enemies. And to decide a question of fact, as well as, of principle, without waiting for such representations and proofs, as the absent and interested party might have to produce would have been a proceeding contrary to the ordinary maxims of justice, and requiring circumstances of a very peculiar nature, to warrant it, towards any nation. Towards a nation which could verify her claim to more than bare justice by our own reiterated and formal acknowledgments, and which must in her present singular and interesting situation have a peculiar sensibility to marks of our friendship or alienation,

[1. Vattel, *Law of Nations.*]

the impropriety of such a proceeding would be infinitely increased, and in the same proportion the improbability of its having taken place.

There are reasons of another sort which would have been a bar to such a proceeding. It would have been as impolitic as it would have been unfair and unkind.

If France meant not to insist on the guaranty, the measure, without giving any present advantage, would have deprived the United States of a future claim which may be of importance to their safety. It would have inspired France with jealousies of a secret bias in this country toward some of her enemies, which might have left in her breast a spirit of contempt and revenge of which the effects might be felt in various ways. It must in particular have tended to inspire her with a disinclination to feed our commerce with those important advantages which it already enjoys, and those more important ones, which it anxiously contemplates. The nation that consumes more of the fruits of our soil than any other nation in the world, and supplies the only foreign raw material of extensive use in the United States would not be unnecessarily provoked by those who understand the public interest, and make it their study, as it is their interest to advance it.

I am aware that the common-place remark will be interposed, that, "commercial privileges are not worth having, when not secured by mutual interest; and never worth purchasing, because they will grow of themselves out of a mutual interest." Prudent men, who do not suffer their reason to be misled by their prejudices will view the subject in a juster light. They will reflect, that if commercial privileges are not worth purchasing, they are worth having without purchase; that in the commerce of a great nation, there are valuable privileges which may be granted or not granted, or granted either to this or that country, without any sensible influence on the interest of the nation itself; that the friendly or unfriendly disposition of a country, is always an article of moment in the calculations of a comprehensive interest; that some sacrifices of interest will be made to other motives; by nations as well as by individuals, though not with the same frequency, or in the same proportions, that more of a disinterested conduct or of a conduct founded on liberal views of interest, prevails in some nations than in others, that as far as can be seen of the influence of the revolution on the genius and the policy of France; particularly with regard to the United States, every thing is to be hoped by the latter on this subject, which one country can reasonably hope from another. In this point of view a greater error could not have been committed than in a step, that might have turned the present disposition of France to open her commerce to us as far as a liberal calculation of her interest would permit, and her friendship towards us, and confidence in our friendship towards her, could prompt, into a disposition to shut it as closely against us as the united motives of interest, of distrust, and of ill-will, could urge her.

On the supposition that France might intend to claim the guaranty, a hasty and harsh refusal before we were asked, on a ground that accused her of being the aggressor in the war against every power in the catalogue of her enemies, and in a crisis when all her sensibility must be alive towards the United States, would have given every possible irritation to a disappointment which every motive that one nation could feel towards another and towards itself, required to be alleviated by all the circumspection and delicacy that could be applied to the occasion.

The silence of the Executive since the accession of Spain and Portugal to the war against France throws great light on the present discussion. Had the proclamation been issued in the sense, and for the purposes ascribed to it, that is to say, as a declaration of neutrality, another would have followed, on that event. If it was the right and duty of the *Government*, that is, the *President*, to manifest to Great Britain and Holland; and to the American merchants and citizens, his *sense*, his *disposition*, and his *views* on the question, whether *the United States were under the circumstances of the case, bound or not, to execute the clause of guaranty, and not to leave it uncertain whether the Executive did or did not believe a state of neutrality,* to be consistent with our treaties, the *duty* as well as the right prescribed a similar manifestation to all the parties concerned after *Spain and Portugal had joined the other

---

* *The writer is betrayed into an acknowledgment of this in his 7th No. where he applies his reasoning to Spain as well as to Great-Britain and Holland. He had forgotten that Spain was not included in the proclamation.*

maritime enemies of France. The opinion of the Executive with respect to a consistency or inconsistency of neutrality with treaties in the *latter case* could not be *inferred* from the proclamation in the former, because the *circumstances might be different.* Taking the proclamation in its proper sense, as reminding all concerned, that as the United States were at peace (that state not being affected by foreign wars, and only to be changed by the legislative authority of the country) the laws of peace were still obligatory and would be enforced, and the inference is so obvious and so applicable to all other cases *whatever circumstances* may distinguish them, that another proclamation would be unnecessary. Here is a new aspect of the whole subject, admonishing us in the most striking manner at once of the danger of the prerogative contended for and the absurdity of the distinctions and arguments employed in its favour. It would be as impossible in practice, as it is in theory, to separate the power of judging and concluding that the obligations of a treaty do not impose war from that of judging and concluding that the obligations *do impose war.* In certain cases, silence would proclaim the latter conclusion, as intelligibly as words could do the former. The writer indeed has himself abandoned the distinction in his VIIth paper, by declaring expressly that the object of the proclamation would have been defeated "by leaving it uncertain whether the Executive did nor *did not* believe a state of neutrality to be consistent with our treaties."

HELVIDIUS

The first issue here is whether the cause of France is truly the cause of liberty or one stained by excesses and extravagances of an unparalleled nature; Hamilton argues that the latter view has a tolerable foundation. The second issue concerns the character of the French regime and whether it would be in the best interests of the United States to ally herself with that regime.

Americanus Number I

[Philadelphia, January 31, 1794]

An examination into the question how far *regard to the cause of liberty* ought to induce the UStates to take part with France in the present war has been promised. This promise shall now be performed; premising only that it is foreign to the immediate object of these papers—a vindication of the Declaration of Neutrality. That *Executive* Act must derive its defence, from a just construction of existing Treaties and Laws. If shewn to be consistent with these the defence is complete.

Whether a mere regard to the cause of Liberty, independent of Treaty, ought to induce us to become *volunteers* in the war is a question, under our constitution, not of Executive, but of Legislative cognizance. It belongs to Congress to say—whether the Nation shall of choice dismiss the olive branch and unfurl the banners of War.

In judging of the eligibility of the measure with a view to the question just stated, it would present itself under two aspects—

I.   Whether the cause of France be truly the cause of liberty, pursued with justice and humanity, and in a manner likely to crown it with honorable success.

Reprinted with permission from *The Papers of Alexander Hamilton*, ed. Harold Syrett et al., vol. 15 (New York: Columbia University Press, 1969), 669–78.

II.   Whether the degree of service, we could render, by participating in the conflict, was likely to compensate, by its utility to the cause, the evils which would probably flow from it to ourselves.

If either of these questions can be answered in the negative, it will result that the consideration, which has been stated, ought not to embark us in the War.

A discussion of the first point will not be entered upon. It would involve an examination too complicated for the compass of these papers; and after all, the subject gives so great scope to opinion, to imagination to feeling that little could be expected from argument. The great leading facts are before the Public; and by this time most men have drawn their conclusions so firmly, that the issue alone can adjust their differences of opinion. There was a time when all men in this Country entertained the same favourable view of the French Revolution. At the present time they all still unite in the wish, that the troubles of France may terminate in the establishment of a free and good government; and all dispassionate well-informed men equally unite in the doubt, whether this is likely to take place under the auspices of those who now govern the affairs of that Country. But agreeing in these two points, there is a great and serious diversity of opinion as to the real merits and probable issue of the French Revolution.

None can deny, that the cause of France has been stained by excesses and extravagances, for which it is not easy, if possible, to find a parallel and at which reason and humanity recoil. Yet many find apologies & extenuations with which they satisfy themselves; they still see in the cause of France the cause of Liberty; they are still sanguine in the hope that it will be crowned with success; that the French Nation will establish for themselves not only a free, but a Republican Government, capable of promoting solidly their happiness. Others on the contrary discern no adequate apology for the horrid and disgusting scenes which have been and continue to be acted. They conceive that the excesses which have been committed transcend greatly the measure of those which were reasonably to have been expected with every due allowance for circumstances. They perceive in them proofs of atrocious depravity in the most influential leaders of the Revolution. They observe, that among these, a Marat and a Robespierre, assassins still reeking with the blood of murdered fellow Citizens, monsters who outdo the fabled enormities of a *Busiris* and a *Procrustes,* are predominent in influence as in iniquity. They find every where marks of an unexampled dissolution of all the social and moral ties. They see no where any thing but principles and opinions so wild so extreme passions so turbulent so tempestuous, as almost to forbid the hope of agreement in any rational or well organised system of Government: They conclude, that a state of things like this is calculated to extend disgust and disaffection throughout the Nation, to nourish more and more a spirit of insurrection and mutiny, facilitating the progress of the invading armies, and exciting in the bowels of France commotions, of which it is impossible to compute the mischiefs the duration or the end: that if by the energy of the national character and the intrinsic difficulty of the enterprise the enemies of France shall be compelled to leave her to herself, this era may only prove the commencement of greater misfortunes: that after wading through seas of blood, in a furious and sanguinary civil war, France may find herself at length the slave of some victorious Scylla or Marius or Caesar: And they draw this afflicting inference from the whole view of the subject, that there is more reason to fear, that the CAUSE OF TRUE LIBERTY has received a deep wound in the mismanagements of it, by those who, unfortunately for the French Nation, have for a considerable time past, maintained an ascendant in its affairs—than to regard the Revolution of France, in the form it has latterly worn, as intitled to the honors due to that sacred and all important cause—or as a safe bark on which to freight the Fortunes the Liberties and the Reputation of this now respectable and happy land.

Without undertaking to determine, which of these opposite opinions rests most firmly on the evidence of facts, I shall content myself with observing that if the latter is conceived to have but a tolerable foundation, it is conclusive against the propriety of our engaging in the war, merely through regard for the cause of Liberty: For when we resolve to put so vast a stake upon the chance of the die, we ought at least to be certain that the object for which we hazard is genuine is substantial is real.

Let us proceed to the discussion of the second question.

To judge of the degree of aid which we could afford to France in her present struggle, it may be of use to take a true view of the means, with which we carried on the War that accomplished our own Revolution.

Our supplies were derived from five sources—1. paper money—2. domestic loans   3. foreign loans   4. pecuniary taxes   5. taxes in specific articles   6. military impress.

The first of these resources with a view to a future war may be put out of the question. Past experience would forbid its being again successfully employed, and no friend to the morals property or industry of the people, to public or private credit, would desire to see it revived.

The second would exist, but probably in a more limited extent. The circumstances of a depreciating paper, which the holders were glad, as they supposed, to realize, was a considerable motive to the loans obtained during the late war. The magnitude of them, however, even then, bore a small proportion to the aggregate expence.

The third resource would be equally out of the question with the first. The principal lending powers would be our enemies as they are now those of France.

The three remaining items—*Pecuniary taxes,* taxes on specific articles; military impress, could be employed again in a future war and are the resources upon which we should have chiefly to rely: for the resources of domestic loans is by no means a very extensive one, in a community where capitals are so moderate as in ours.

Though it is not to be doubted, that the People of the UStates would hereafter as heretofore throw their whole property into common stock for their common defence against internal invasion or an unprovoked attack—who is there sanguine enough to believe that large contributions either in money or produce could be extracted from them to carry on an external war voluntarily undertaken for a foreign and speculative purpose?

The expectation were an illusion. Those who may entertain it ought to pause and reflect. Whatever enthusiasm might have been infused into a part of the community would quickly yield to more just and sober ideas inculcated by experience of the burthens & calamities of war. The circuitous logic, by which it is attempted to be maintained, that a participation in the war is necessary to the security of our own liberty would then appear, as it truly is, a mere delusion, propagated by bribed incendiaries or hairbrained enthusiasts. And the authors of the delusion would not fail to be execrated as the enemies of the public weal.

Viewing the matter dispassionately, we cannot but conclude, that in a war of *choice*, not of *necessity*, like that in which we are invited to engage—it would be a bad calculation to look for great exertions of the community.

The business would move as heavily, as it was in its origin impolitic. The faculty of the government to obtain pecuniary supplies would in such a situation be circumscribed within a narrow compass. Levies of men would not be likely to be more successful than those of money. No one would think of detaching the Militia for distant expeditions abroad: And the experience we have had in our Indian enterprizes do not authorise strong expectations of going far, by voluntary enlistments, where the question is not as it was during the last war the defence of the essential rights & interests of the Country. The severe expedient of drafting from the Militia, a principal reliance in that war, would put the authority of Government in the case supposed to a very critical test.

This summary view of what would be our situation & prospects is alone sufficient to demonstrate the general position that our ability to promote the cause of France by external exertions could not be such as to be very material to the event.

Let us however for more complete elucidation inquire to what particular objects they could be directed.

Fleets we have not and could not have in time or to an extent to be of use in the contest.

Shall we raise an army and send it to France? She does not want soldiers. Her own population can amply furnish her armies. The number we could send, if we could get them there at all, would be of no weight in the scale.

The true wants of France are of system, order, money, provisions, arms, military stores.

System and Order we could not give her by engaging in the war. The supply of money in that event would be out of our power. At present we can pay our debt to her in proportion as it becomes due. Then we could not even do this. Provisions and other supplies, as far as we are in condition to furnish them, could not then be furnished at all. The conveyance of them would become more difficult — & the forces we should be obliged ourselves to raise would consume our surplus.

Abondonning then, as of necessity we must, the idea of aiding France in Europe, shall we turn our attention to the succour of her Islands? Alas we should probably have here only to combat their own internal disorders to aid Frenchmen against French men—whites against blacks, or blacks against whites. If we may judge from the past conduct of the powers at war with France their effort is immediately against herself—her Islands are not in the first instance, a serious object. But grant that they become so, is it evident, that we can cooperate efficaciously to their preservation? Or if we can what will this have to do with the preservation of French Liberty. The dangers to this arise, from the invasion of foreign armies carried into the bosom of France—from the still more formidable assaults of civil dissention and the spirit of anarchy.

Shall we attack the Islands of the Powers opposed to France?

How shall we without a competent fleet carry on the necessary expeditions for the purpose? Where is such a fleet? How shall we maintain our conquests after they are made? What influence could the capture of an Island or two have upon the general issue of the Contest? These questions answer themselves.

Or Shall we endeavour to make a diversion in favour of France by attacking canada on the one side & Florida on the other?

This certainly would be the most, indeed the only, eligible mode of aiding France in war. These enterprises may be considered as within the compass of our means.

But while this is admitted, it ought not to be regarded as a very easy task. The reduction of Canada ought not to be undertaken with less than   men; that of the Floridas with much fewer than   [1] for reinforcement could be brought to both those countries from the West India possessions of their respective sovereigns. Relying on their naval superiority, they could spare from the Islands all the troops which were not necessary to the preservation of their internal tranquillity.

These armies are then to be raised and equipped and to be provided with all the requisite apparatus for operation. Proportionate magazines are to be formed for their accommodation and supply.

Some men, whose fate it is to think loosely may imagine that a more summary substitute could be found in the Mi[li]tia. But the Militia, an excellent auxiliary for internal defence, could not be advantageously employed in distant expeditions requiring time and perseverance. For these, men regularly engaged for a competent period are indispensable. The conquest of Canada at least may with decision be regarded as out of the reach of a Militia operation.

If war was resolved upon, the very preparation of the means for the enterprizes which have been mentioned would demand not less than a year. Before this period was elapsed, the fate of France, as far as foreign invasion is concerned, would probably be decided. It would be manifest either that she could or could not be subjugated by force of external coertion. Our interposition would therefore be too late to benefit her. It appears morally certain, that the War against France cannot be of much duration. The Exertions are too mighty to be long protracted.

The only way in which the enterprizes in question could serve the cause of France would be by making a diversion of a part of those forces which would otherwise be directed against her. But this consequence could not be counted upon. It would be known that we could not be very early ready to attack with effect; and it would be an obvious policy to risk secondary objects rather than be diverted from the efficacious pursuit of the main one. It would be natural in such case to rely for indemnification on the successful result of

[1. The blank spaces contain numbers that were crossed out by Hamilton.]

the War in Europe. The Governments concerned imagine that they have too much at stake upon that result not to hazard considerably elsewhere in order to secure the fairest chance of its being favourable to their wishes.

It would not probably render the matter better, to precipitate our measures for the sake of a more speedy impulse. The parties ought in such case to count upon the abortion of our attempts from their immaturity, and to rely the more confidently upon the means of resistance already on the spot.

We could not therefore flatter ourselves that the expedient last proposed—that of attacking the possessions of Great Britain and Spain in our neighbourhood—would be materially serviceable to the cause of France.

But to give the argument its fairest course, I shall take notice of two particulars, in respect to which our interference would be more sensibly felt. These are the depredations, which our privateers might make upon the commerce of the maritime enemies of France, and the direct injury which would accrue to that of G Britain from the interruption of intercourse between the two Countries. Considering the shock lately sustained by mercantile credit in that Country—the real importance to it of our imports from thence and of our exports thither, the large sums which are due and in a continual course of remittance from our merchants to her Merchants—a war between the UStates and Great Britain could not fail to be seriously distressing to her.

Yet it would be weak to count upon very decisive influence of these circumstances. The Public credit of G Britain has still energy sufficient to enable her to struggle with much partial derangement. Her private credit manifestly disordered by temporary causes, and propped as it has been by the public purse seems to have recovered its impaired tone. Her commerce too suddenly interrupted by the breaking out of war must have resumed its wonted channels in proportion as the progress of her naval preparations has tended to give it protection. And though the being at war with us would be very far from a matter of indifference either to her commerce or to her credit; yet it is not likely that it would arrest her carreer or overrule those paramount considerations which brought her into her present situation.

When we recollect how she maintained herself under a privation of our commerce, through a seven years war with us, united for certain periods of it with France Spain & Holland, though we perceive a material difference between her present and her then situation arising from that very effort, yet we cannot reasonably doubt that she would be able notwithstanding a similar privation to continue a war which in fact does not call for an equal exertion on her part, as long as the other powers with which she is associated shall be in condition to prosecute it with a hope of success. Nor is it probable, whatever may be the form or manner of the engagement, that Great Britain could, if disposed to peace, honorably make a separate retreat. It is the interest of all parties in such cases to assure to each other a cooperation: and it is presumeable that this has taken place in some shape or other between the Powers at present combined against France.

The conclusion from the several considerations which have been presented carefully & dispassionately weighed is this, that there is no probable prospect of this country rendering material service to the cause of France, by engaging with her in the War.

It has been very truly observed in the course of the publications, upon the subject—*that if France is not in some way or other wanting to herself she will not stand in need of our assistance and if she is our assistance cannot save her.*

PACIFICUS

Hamilton is reiterating the possible consequences (both commercial and
military) of joining France in her war with England, focusing especially
on the attitude of those European powers confederated against France.
Such a war would interrupt the prosperity of the United States.

Americanus Number II

[Philadelphia, February 7, 1794]

Let us now turn to the other side of the medal. To be struck with it, it is
not necessary to exaggerate.

All who are not wilfully blind must see and acknowlege that this Country at present enjoys an unexampled state of prosperity. That war would
interrupt it need not be affirmed. We should then by war lose the advantage
of that astonishing progress in strength wealth and improvement, which
we are now making, and which if continued for a few years will place our
national rights and interests upon immoveable foundations. This loss alone
would be of infinite moment: it is such a one as no prudent or good man
would encounter but for some clear necessity or some positive duty.

If while Europe is exhausting herself in a destructive war, this country
can maintain its peace, the issue will open to us a wide field of advantages,
which even imagination can with difficulty compass.

But a check to the *progress* of our prosperity is not the greatest evil to be
anticipated. Considering the naval superiority of the enemies of France we
cannot doubt that our commerce would be in a great degree annihilated by
a war. Our Agriculture would of course with our commerce receive a deep
wound. The exportations which now contribute to animate it could not fail

Reprinted with permission from *The Papers of Alexander Hamilton,* ed. Harold Syrett
et al., vol. 16 (New York: Columbia University Press, 1972), 12–19.

to be essentially diminished. Our mechanics would experience their full share of the common calamity. That lively and profitable industry which now sp[r]eads a smile over all our cities and Towns would feel an instantaneous and rapid decay.

Nine tenths of our present revenues are derived from commercial duties. Their declension must of course keep pace with that of Trade. A substitute cannot be found in other sources of taxation, without imposing heavy burthens on the People. To support public credit and carry on the war would suppose exactions really grievous. To abandon public Credit would be to renounce an essential means of carrying on the war, besides the sacrifice of the public Creditors and the disgrace of a National bankruptcy.

We will not call in the aid of Savage butcheries and depredations to heighten the picture. Tis enough to say, that a general Indian War, incited by the united influence of Britain and Spain, would not fail to spread desolation throughout our frontier.

To a people who have so recently and so severely felt the evils of War little more is necessary, than to appeal to their own recollection for their magnitude and extent.

The war which now rages is & for obvious reasons is likely to continue to be carried on with unusual animosity and rancour. It is highly probable that the resentment of the combined powers against us if we should take part in the war would be if possible still more violent than it is against France. Our interference would be regarded as altogether officious and wanton. How far this idea might lead to an aggravation of the ordinary calamities of war would deserve serious reflection.

The certain evils of our joining France in the war are sufficient dissuasives from so intemperate a measure. The possible ones are of a nature to call for all our caution, all our prudence.

To defend its own rights, to vindicate its own honor, there are occasions when a Nation ought to hazard even its existence. Should such an occasion occur, I trust those who are now most averse to commit the peace of the country will not be the last to face the danger, nor the first to turn their backs upon it.

But let us at least have the consolation of not having rashly courted misfortune. Let us have to act under the animating reflection of being engaged in repelling wrongs which we neither sought nor merited, in vindicating our rights, invaded without provocation, in defending our honor violated without cause. Let us not have to reproach ourselves with having voluntarily bartered blessings for calamities.

But we are told that our own Liberty is at stake upon the event of the war against France—that if she falls we shall be the next victim. The combined powers, it is said, will never forgive in us the origination of those principles which were the germs of the French Revolution. They will endeavour to eradicate them from the world.

If this suggestion were ever so well founded, it would perhaps be a sufficient answer to it to say, that our interference is not likely to alter the case—that it could only serve prematurely to exhaust our strength.

But other answers more conclusive present themselves.

The war against France requires on the part of her enemies efforts unusually violent. They are obliged to strain every nerve, to exert every resource. However it may terminate, they must find themselves spent in an extreme degree; a situation not very favourable to the undertaking a new, and even to Europe combined, an immense enterprize.

To subvert by force republican Liberty in this Country, nothing short of entire conquest would suffice. This conquest, with our present increased population; greatly distant as we are from Europe, would either be impracticable or would demand such exertions, as following immediately upon those which will have been requisite to the subversion of the French Revolution, would be absolutely ruinous to the undertakers.

It is against all probability, that an undertaking, pernicious as this would be, even in the event of success, would be attempted against an unoffending Nation by its Geographical position, so little connected with the political concerns of Europe.

But impediments would arise from more special causes. Suppose France subdued, and a restoration of the Monarchy in its ancient form or a partition effected. To uphold either state of things, after the general impulse in favour of liberty, which has been given to the minds of 24 Millions of people, would in one way or another find occupation for a considerable part of the forces which had brought it about. In the event of an unqualified restoration of the monarchy if the future monarch did not stand in need of foreign legions for the support of his authority; still the Powers who had been concerned in the restoration could not sufficiently rely upon the solidity of the order of things reestablished by them not to keep themselves in a posture to be prepared against the disturbance of it—'till there had been time to compose the discordant interests and passions produced by the Revolution and bring back the Nation to ancient habits of subordination. In the event of a partition of France, it would of course give occupation to the forces of the conquerors to secure the submission of the dismembered parts.

The new dismemberment of Poland will be another obstacle to the detaching of troops from Europe for a crusade against this Country. The fruits of that transaction can only be secured to Russia and Prussia by the agency of large bodies of forces kept on foot for the purpose within the dismembered territories.

Of the powers combined against France there are only three whose interests have any material reference to this Country—England, Spain, Holland.

As to Holland it will be readily conceded that she can have no interest or feeling to induce her to embark in so mad & wicked a project. Let us see how the matter will stand with regard to Spain & England.

The object of the enterprise against us must either be the establishment in this Country of a royal in place of our present Republican Government, the subjugation of the Country to the dominion of one of the parties, or its division among them.

The establish[men]t of an independent monarchy in this country would be so manifestly against the interests of both those Nations, in the ordinary acceptation of this term in politics—that neither of them can be so absurd as to desire it.

It may be adopted as an axiom in our political calculation, that no foreign power which has valuable colonies in America will be propitious to our remaining one people united under a vigorous Government.

No man I believe but will think it probable, however disadvantageous the change in other respects, that a Monarchical Government, from its superior force, would ensure more effectually than our present form our permanent unity as a Nation. This at least would be the indubitable conclusion of European calculators. From which may be confidently inferred a disinclination both in England and Spain to our undergoing a change of that kind.

The only thing that can be imagined capable of reconciling either of those Powers to it would be the giving us for monarch a member of its own royal family and forming something like a family compact.

But here would arise a direct collision of interest between them. Which of them would agree that a prince of the family of the other should be reigning over this country and give to that other a decided preponderancy in the scale of American affairs?

The subjugation of the UStates to the dominion of either of those Powers would fall more strongly under a like consideration. Tis impossible that either of them should consent that the other should become Master of this Country—And neither of them without madness could desire a mastery which would cost more than 'twas worth to maintain it, and which from an irresistible course of things could be but of very short duration.

The third, namely the division of it between them, is the most colorable of the three suppositions—But even this would be the excess of folly in both.

Nothing could be more unwise, in the first instance, in Great Britain, than to consent by that measure to divide with Spain the emoluments of our Commerce which now in so great a degree center with her with a probability of continuing to do it as long as the natural relations of commerce are permitted to govern.

Spain too could not fail to be sensible that from obvious causes her dominion over the part which was allotted to her would be altogether transient.

The first collision between Britain and Spain would certainly have one of two effects—either a reunion of the whole Country under Great Britain or a dismission of the yoke of both.

The latter by far the most probable would discover to both the extreme absurdity of the project.

The UStates, rooted as are now the ideas of Independence, are happily too remote from Europe to be governed by her. Dominion over any part of them would be a real misfortune to any Nation of that Quarter of the Globe.

To Great Britain the enterprise supposed would threaten serious consequences in more ways than one. It may safely be affirmed that she would run by it greater risk of bankruptcy and Revolution than we of subjugation. A chief proportion of the burthen would unavoidably fall upon her as the most monied & principal maritime power & it may emphatically be said that she would make war upon her own commerce & credit. There is the strongest ground to believe that the Nation would disrelish and oppose the project. The certainty of great evils attending it—the dread of much greater—experience of the disasters of the last war would operate upon all. Many, not improbably a majority, would see in the enterprise a malicious and wanton hostility against Liberty, of which they might themselves expect to be the next victim. Their judgments and their feelings would easily distinguish this case from that either of their former contest with us or their present contest with France. In the former, they had pretensions to support which were plausible enough to mislead their pride and their interest. In the latter, there were strong circumstances to rouse their passions alarm their fears and induce an acquiescence in the course which was pursued.

But a future attack upon us, as apprehended, would be so absolutely pretextless, as not to be misunderstood. Our conduct will have been such as to intitle us to the reverse of unfriendly or hostile dispositions: While powerful motives of self-interest would advocate with them our cause.

But Britain Spain Austria Prussia and perhaps even Russia will have more need and a stronger desire of peace & repose to restore and recruit their wasted strength and exhausted Treasuries—to reinvigorate the interior order and industry of their respective kingdoms relaxed and depressed by war—than either means or inclination to undertake so extravagant an enterprise against the Liberty of this Country.

If there can be any danger to us of that sort it must arise from our voluntarily thrusting ourselves into the War. Once embarked, Nations sometimes prosecute enterprises which they would not otherwise have dreamt of. The most violent resentment would no doubt in such case be kindled against us for what would be called a wanton and presumptuous intermeddling on our part. What this might produce it is not easy to calculate.

There are too great errors in our reasoning upon this subject. One is that the combined Powers will certainly attribute to us the same principles which they deem so exceptionable in France; the other, that our principles are in fact the same.

If left to themselves, they will all except one naturally see in us a people who originally resorted to a Revolution in Governt as a refuge from encroachment on rights and privileges *antecedently* enjoyed—not as a people who from choice have sought a radical and intire change in the established Government, in pursuit of new privileges and rights carried to an extreme, not reconciliable perhaps with any form of regular Government. They will see in us a people who have a due respect for property and personal security—who in the midst of our revolution abstained with exemplary moderation from every thing violent or sanguinary instituting governments adequate to the protection of persons and property; who since the completion of our revolution have in a very short period, from mere reasoning and reflection, without tumult or bloodshed adopted a form of general Government calculated as well as the nature of things would permit—to remedy antecedent defects—to give strength and security to the Nation—to rest the foundations of Liberty on the basis of Justice Order and Law—who at all times have been content to govern ourselves; unmeddling in the Governments or Affairs of other Nations: in fine, they will see in us sincere Republicans but decided enemies to licentiousness and anarchy—sincere republicans but decided friends to the freedom of opinion, to the order and tranquility of all Mankind. They will not see in us a people whose best passions have been misled and whose best qualities have been perverted from their true aim by headlong fanatical or designing leaders to the perpetration of acts from which humanity shrinks—to the commission of outrages, over which the eye of reason weeps—to the profession and practice of principles which tend to shake the foundations of morality—to dissolve the social bands—to disturb the peace of mankind—to substitute confusion to order anarchy to Government.

Such at least is the light in which the Reason or the passions of the Powers confederated against France lead them to view her principles and conduct. And it is to be lamented that so much cause has been given for their opinions. If on our part, we give no incitement to their passions, facts too prominent and too decisive to be combated will forbid their reason to bestow the same character upon us.

It is therefore matter of real regret that there should be an effort on our part to level the distinctions, which discriminate our case from that of France—to confound the two cases in the view of foreign powers—and to hazard our own principles, by persuading ourselves of a similitude which does not exist.

Let us content ourselves with lamenting the errors into which a great, a gallant, an amiable a respectable Nation has been betrayed—with uniting our wishes and our prayers that the Supreme Ruler of the World will bring them back from those errors to a more sober and more just way of think⟨ing⟩ and acting and will overrule the complicated calamities which surround them to the establishment of a Government under which they may be free secure and happy. But let us not corrupt ourselves by false comparisons or glosses—nor shut our eyes to the true nature of transactions which ought to grieve and warn us—not rashly mingle our destiny in the consequences of the errors and extravagances of another nation.

PACIFICUS

Index

ambassadors: power to receive, 14–15, 74–83. *See also* minister of French Republic

American possessions of France: Treaty of Alliance with France only covering, 27–28; U.S. ability to aid France regarding, 104–5, 106

American Revolution: disparity of circumstances compared with French war against European powers, 44; gratitude for French assistance with (*see* gratitude to France); resources of Great Britain and, 107; resources used in pursuit of, 102

appointment and removal powers, xii–xiii, 57, 62–63

Austria, 48, 113

Burlamaqui, Jean-Jacques, 20, 58, 78

Canada, 104–5. *See also* American possessions of France

changes in government. *See* revolutions of government

Clause of Guarantee. *See* France, Treaty of Alliance with

commander in chief, president as, 61–62

concurrent or overlapping spheres of power, xii, xiv, 60–61, 66–70

conquered territories, rights regarding, 24–25

Constitution: ambassadors, power to receive, 75; characterization by Hamilton of motives of critics of Neutrality Proclamation regarding, 3, 6–7; on declarations of war, 60, 67, 68; general grant of executive powers by, viii–ix, 12–17; new principles and constructions, Hamilton accused by Madison of introducing, xiii, 84–98; separation of powers principle, x, xiv, 60–61, 66–70; significance of Pacificus-Helvidius debates for, xiii–xiv; strict construction by Madison, 60–64, 84–89; on treaties, 61; as unfinished/open-ended, vii–viii, xiv

diplomatic representatives: power to receive, 14–15, 74–83. *See also* minister of French Republic

disposition of United States, power of president to declare, 52–53, 93

executive powers, viii–x; ambassadors, power to receive, 14–15, 74–83; appointment and removal powers, xii–xiii, 57, 62–63; commander in chief, president as, 61–62;

executive powers (*continued*)
Constitution's general grant of,
viii–ix, 12–17, 61–63; dangerous
implications of Neutrality
Proclamation regarding, 90–98;
disposition of United States, power
of president to declare, 52–53,
93; exceptions and qualifications
regarding, 13–16, 56–57, 66;
government as term applied
exclusively to, 90–91; peace, power
to make, 87–89; peace and neutrality,
maintenance of state of, 71–73,
92–93; positions of Hamilton and
Madison on, viii–xiv; separation
of powers principle, x, xiv, 60–61,
66–70; significance of Pacificus-
Helvidius debates for defining,
xiii–xiv; strict construction of, 55–64,
84–89; treaties, x–xiii, 13–14, 55–64,
74–75; war, power of making, 55–64.
See also foreign affairs, power over

Federalist Papers: on ambassadors, 76;
Pacificus-Helvidius debates viewed as
supplement to, xv; on treaty-making
powers, xi, 63–64, 88
federative power, xi
Floridas, 104–5. *See also* American
possessions of France
foreign affairs, power over, vii, viii,
ix–x; ambassadors, power to
receive, 14–15, 74–83; defensive
alliances *vs.* offensive wars, 18–25;
essential nature of foreign affairs
for purposes of, xiii, 11–12, 55–64;
significance of Pacificus-Helvidius
debates for defining, xiii–xiv; specific
rights granted to legislative power
regarding, 13–16. *See also* treaties;
war, power of making
foreign attachments: Hamilton on need
to guard against, 46–47; Madison on
need to consult with, 94–97

France: address announcing
appointment of minister
plenipotentiary, intimations
regarding American Revolution
in, 44–46; American possessions
of, 27–28, 104–5, 106; character of
current regime, consideration of,
38–43, 99–107; decrees on liberty
issued by, 22–24. *See also* gratitude to
France; minister of French Republic
France, Treaty of Alliance with:
American possessions of France
only covered by, 27–28; Neutrality
Proclamation at odds with Clause of
Guarantee in, 10, 18; offensive wars
not engaging defensive alliance of,
18–25
Franklin, Benjamin, 39
French Revolution: Hamilton on, 4, 25,
29, 40, 100–101; Madison on, 55
French war with European powers:
ability of United States to assist
with, 26–29, 44, 49, 102–7; dangers
of United States to involvement in,
107–15; disparity of circumstances
compared with American Revolution,
44; nefarious motives of critics of
Neutrality Proclamation and, 1, 4,
7; as offensive war not engaging
defensive alliance, 18–25; request
of belligerent powers, Neutrality
Proclamation issued without, 50–
51, 94; self-preservation in face of,
American duty of, 26–29, 102–
15; time and date of issuance of
Neutrality Proclamation, reasons for,
48–50, 97–98; whether liberty may be
regarded as cause of, 99–101, 110–12

government as term applied to executive
authority alone, 90–91
gratitude to France, 30; disparity of
circumstances affecting, 44; Louis
XVI and, 37–43, 45; moral duty of

gratitude, nations not subject to, 32–34; motives of France regarding assistance in American Revolution and, 35–40, 44–46; self-preservation and self-interest *versus,* 32–33 (*see also* self-preservation and self-interest, national duty of)

Great Britain: American possessions of, 104–5, 106; French rivalry as grounds for their assistance in American Revolution, 35–40; interests regarding United States, 111–15; resources for continuing war, 106–7; royal prerogatives, making war and treaties as, 63; statements of French President of National Convention naturally alarming to, 23–24; time and date of issuance of Neutrality Proclamation, reasons for, 48, 97

Hamilton, Alexander: on character of current French regime, 38–43, 99–107; on defensive alliances *vs.* offensive wars, 18–25; foreign affairs, power of government most fit to control, 11; foreign attachments, need to guard against, 46–47; general grant of executive powers in Constitution, inferences drawn from, viii–ix, 12–17; on gratitude (*see* gratitude to France); initial defense of Neutrality Proclamation by, vii–viii, 2–7; on involvement of United States in French war with European powers, 102–15; on liberty as cause (*see* liberty); on Louis XVI, 37–40, 41–42; on nature and design of Neutrality Proclamation, 9–10; on nefarious motives of those criticizing Neutrality Proclamation, 2–7, 8–9; new principles and constructions, Hamilton accused by Madison of introducing, xiii, 84–98; peace, consistency of Neutrality Proclamation with preservation of, 30–32; portrait of, ii; position of, viii–xiv; on prudence of issuing Neutrality Proclamation, 48–53; on self-preservation and self-interest (*see* self-preservation and self-interest, national duty of)

Holland, 22, 48, 97, 111

Hopkins, George F., xv

Jefferson, Thomas: criticism of Neutrality proclamation by, vii–viii; instigation of Madison to debate with Hamilton by, viii, 54

judicial powers: concurrent or overlapping spheres of power, 69; control of foreign affairs not proper to, 11; treaties, suspension of terms of, 79–80

La Fayette, Marquis de, 40

legislative powers: peace, power to make, 87–89; separation of powers principle, x, xiv, 60–61, 66–70; strict construction of, 60–64, 84–89; treaties, x–xiii, 13–14, 55–64, 74–75; war, power of making, 65–73, 93–94. *See also* foreign affairs, power over

liberty: duty to assist cause of, 43; French decrees on, natural alarm arising from, 22–24; French war with European powers and cause of, 99–101, 110–14

Locke, John, xi, 58

Louis XVI, 37–43, 45

Madison, James: on ambassadors, 14–15, 74–83; on blocking of legislative power to declare war by Neutrality Proclamation, 65–73, 93–94; on dangerous implications of Neutrality Proclamation, 90–98; foreign attachments, need to consult with,

Madison, James (*continued*)
94–97; Jefferson, instigation to
debate with Hamilton by, viii, 54;
new principles and constructions,
Hamilton accused by Madison of
introducing, xiii, 84–98; portrait
of, ii; position of, viii–xiv; on
revolutions of government, 78–83;
on strict construction of executive
powers regarding war and treaties,
55–64, 84–89
Marat, Jean-Paul, 101
minister of French Republic: address
announcing appointment,
intimations regarding American
Revolution in, 44–46; failure to
consult with, 48, 50, 94–97; Jefferson
on, 54
monarchies: making war and treaties
as royal prerogatives, 63, 88–89;
opinions of jurists based on
observation of, 57–59
Montesquieu, Charles Louis de
Secondat, Baron de, 58
moral standards, national applicability
of, 32–34
mutual interest as basis for international
relations, 32–33, 96

navy of United States, infant state of, 26,
27, 44, 103
Netherlands. *See* Holland
neutrality: executive responsibility to
maintain state of, 71–73, 92–93;
peace, as equivalent of, 71
Neutrality Proclamation of 1793: effect
of, vii; French Treaty of Alliance
terms affected by, 10; Hamilton's
initial defense of, vii–viii, 2–7;
legislature's power to declare war
blocked by, 65–73, 93–94; Madison
on dangerous implications of,
90–98; minister of French Republic,
failure to consult with, 48, 50,
94–97; nature and design of, 9–10;

nefarious motives of those criticizing,
Hamilton on, 2–7, 8–9; objections
to, Hamilton's list of, 9; peace,
consistency with preservation of,
30–32; prudence of issuing, 48–53;
request of belligerent powers, issued
without, 50–51, 94; text of, 1; time
and date of issuance, reasons for,
48–50, 97–98; treaty conditions,
failure to address, 51–52
new principles and constructions on
Constitution, Hamilton accused
by Madison of introducing, xiii,
84–98

Pacificus-Helvidius debates, vii–xiv;
arguments and positions involved in,
viii–xiii; Constitutional significance
of, xiii–xiv; *Federalist Papers,* as
supplement to, xv
peace: consistency of Neutrality
Proclamation with preservation of,
30–32, 50; executive responsibility to
maintain state of, 71–73; neutrality
as equivalent of, 71; power to make,
87–89
Poland, 111
Portugal, 97
presidency. *See* executive powers
proclamations, nature of, 92
prudence of issuing Neutrality
Proclamation, 48–53
Prussia, 48, 111, 113
public rights, 79–81
Pufendorf, Samuel, 29n

reciprocal advantage as basis for
international relations, 32–33, 96
removal and appointment powers,
xii–xiii, 57, 62–63
revolutions of government: ambassadors,
power of receiving, 76–83; treaty
terms and, 29, 78–83. *See also*
American Revolution; French
Revolution

Robespierre, Maximilien, 101
Russia, 111, 113
Saratoga, victories of, 36
self-preservation and self-interest,
national duty of: foreign attachments,
need to guard against, 46–47; French
cause, wisdom of involvement in,
26–29, 102–15; gratitude compared,
32–33; liberty, assisting cause of,
43; motives of France regarding
assistance in American Revolution
and, 35–40, 44–46; as reason for
issuance of Neutrality Proclamation,
26–29; reciprocal advantage and
mutual interest as best basis for
international relations, 32–33, 96
separation of powers principle, x, xiv,
60–61, 66–70
Society for constitutional information in
London, 23
Spain: American possessions of, 104–5,
106; in American Revolution, 44;
interests regarding United States,
111–15; time and date of issuance of
Neutrality Proclamation, reasons
for, 48, 97

treaties: ambassadors, significance of
power to receive, 14–15, 74–83;
Constitution on, 61; defensive
alliances vs. offensive wars, 18–25;
executive and legislative powers
regarding, x–xiii, 13–14, 55–64,
74–75, 85–89; failure of Neutrality
Proclamation to address, 51–52;
Federalist Papers on, xi, 63–64; Great

Britain, as royal prerogative in, 63;
jurists, opinions of, 57–59; nature and
design of Neutrality Proclamation
regarding terms of, 9–10; revolutions
of government and terms of, 29,
78–83. See also France, Treaty of
Alliance with

United States: critics of Neutrality
Proclamation as desirous of
overturning, 2–7; dangers of
involvement in French war to, 107–
15; disposition of, power of president
to declare, 52–53, 93; strength and
condition of, 26–29, 44, 49, 102–7.
See also American Revolution

Vattel, Emmerich de, 10n, 23, 28, 58, 78,
94, 95

war, power of making: ambassadors,
power of receiving, 76–83;
Constitution on, 60, 67, 68; Great
Britain, as royal prerogative in, 63;
jurists, opinions of, 57–59; legislative
vs. executive nature of, 55–64,
84–89; Neutrality Proclamation as
blocking legislature's exercise of,
65–73, 93–94
Washington, George: Hamilton's
defense of character and public
esteem of, 6; Neutrality Proclamation
(see Neutrality Proclamation of 1793)
West Indies, 27–28, 104–5. See also
American possessions of France
Wolfius (Christian von Wolff), 58

The typeface used in this book is Adobe Caslon, a 1990 interpretation by Carol Twombly of the classic face cut in the 1720s by the English typographer William Caslon (1692–1766). Trained as an engraver, Caslon turned to type design and cutting, setting up his own type foundry in 1720. Caslon's became the first major native English typeface to achieve wide popularity. It displays the small lowercase height and the restrained contrast typical of what are now called old-style fonts. The modern version smooths out many of the idiosyncrasies of William Caslon's original cutting, while retaining the warmth and honesty that have made Caslon a friend of the typographer for centuries.

This book is printed on paper that is acid-free
and meets the requirements of the American National Standard
for Permanence of Paper for Printed Library Materials,
z39.48-1992. ∞

Book design by Mark McGarry, Texas Type and Book Works, Inc., Dallas, Texas
Typography by G&S Typesetters, Inc., Austin, Texas
Printed and bound by Edwards Brothers, Inc., Ann Arbor, Michigan